Titles in the 'Island Tribute' Series
The Isle of Mull
The Island of Staffa
The Isle of Iona

British Library
Cataloguing-in-publication data.
A catalogue record for this book is available
from the British Library.

ISBN   0 9521517 5 8   *(paperback)*
ISBN   0 9521517 6 6   *(hardback)*
© Alastair de Watteville, 1999

Published by:
Romsey Fine Art
P O Box 28, Romsey,
Hampshire SO51 0ZF

Designed by:
Pierrot Print & Design Ltd
Badshot Farm, Badshot Lea, Farnham,
Surrey GU9 9HY

Printed by:
Fenn Print
77 Alexandra Road, Farnborough,
Hampshire GU14 6BN

*Opposite page: View from the north of Iona,
across the Sound of Iona, to high ground on Mull*

Outside Cover, Main Picture *(and repeated above): View over The Port of the Coracle,
looking south-east. The Paps of Jura can just be made out
on the horizon on the far left*
Outside Cover, Inset *(and repeated, top): MacLean's Cross, which stands just outside
the parish church, seen from the east*
Endpapers: *reproduction of ancient Pictish key pattern*

THE ISLE OF
IONA

THE ISLE OF IONA

SACRED · SPECTACULAR · LIVING

A Tribute in Photographs, Paintings, Drawings, Maps and Words

ALASTAIR DE WATTEVILLE

ROMSEY R FINE ART

The publishers are extremely grateful to the individuals and organisations named below for making available the images in whatever form to provide the illustrations for this book.

(The numbers below refer to the picture captions. FP1, FP2 and FP3 refer to the front pages of the 'Sacred Island', 'Spectacular Island' and 'Living Island' parts of the book.)

Photographs

Air Images   48, 167, 188

John Alexander   Outside cover and inset, 3, 6, 15, 26, 28, 33, 34, 46, 62, 65, 73, 79, 86, 92, 132, FP3, 165, 174, 183, 190

Edinburgh Photographic Library   36, 41, 93, 191

Graham Ellis   177, 178

The Glasgow Herald   75

John Mann   Half-title page, 5, 27, 58, 83

National Galleries of Scotland   53, 54, 56, 71

National Museums of Scotland   16, 37, 44, 156, 158, 159, 176, 189

The National Trust for Scotland   1, 29, 35, 47, 64, 67, 72, FP2, 80, 84, 85, 137, 160, 168, 170, 171, 173, 175,181

Oxford Scientific Films   94, 96-131, 134-136, 138-143, 145, 147, 149, 150, 152-155

The Royal Commission on the Ancient and Historic Monuments of Scotland   30, 32, 38, 45, 52, 55, 57, 63

The Still Moving Picture Company   21, 25, 39, 40, 70, 74, 78, 81, 157, 169

The University of Dublin   Fronticepiece, 7, 13, 14

Estlin Waters   FP1, 12, 43, 49, 132, 144, 146, 148, 151, 161, 185, 196

Alastair de Watteville   2, 4, 8, 9, 11, 18, 31, 66, 68, 69, 76, 77, 88, 89, 90, 91, 162-164, 166, 179, 180, 182, 184, 186, 187, 193, 195

Paintings

Jan Fisher   95, 194

Pat Malpas   42

Gordon Menzies   87

Tom Shanks   24

Julia Wroughton   172

Fronticepiece (previous left hand page): A detail from the Book of Kells, folio 130r. The page is reproduced in its entirety on page 19

CONTENTS

Acknowledgements 6

Foreword 9
by Trevor Croft,
Director, The National Trust for Scotland

IONA: Sacred Island

1. Early Days on Iona 12
2. Saint Columba 16
3. Viking Raids 24
4. The Benedictine Abbey 28
5. The Nunnery 36
6. Silent Years 42
7. Rebuilding the Abbey Church 50
8. George MacLeod
   and the Iona Community 54

The Revd Norman Shanks, Leader of the
Iona Community, contributed to Chapter 8.

IONA: Spectacular Island

9. The Island and its Outliers 62
10. The Land and the Shore 66
11. Flowers 72
12. Marine Life 78
13. Birds 82

Professor Estlin Waters contributed
Chapter 13.

IONA: Living Island

14. The Population of Iona 94
15. Island Activities 98
16. The Nuts & Bolts
    of Island Life 110
17. Trying to Look Ahead 112

MAPS

Physical map of Iona 8
Viking Sea-routes 26
The Geology of Iona 65
Bird-watching Areas 82

Related Reading 116

The Artists 118

Index 122

IONA

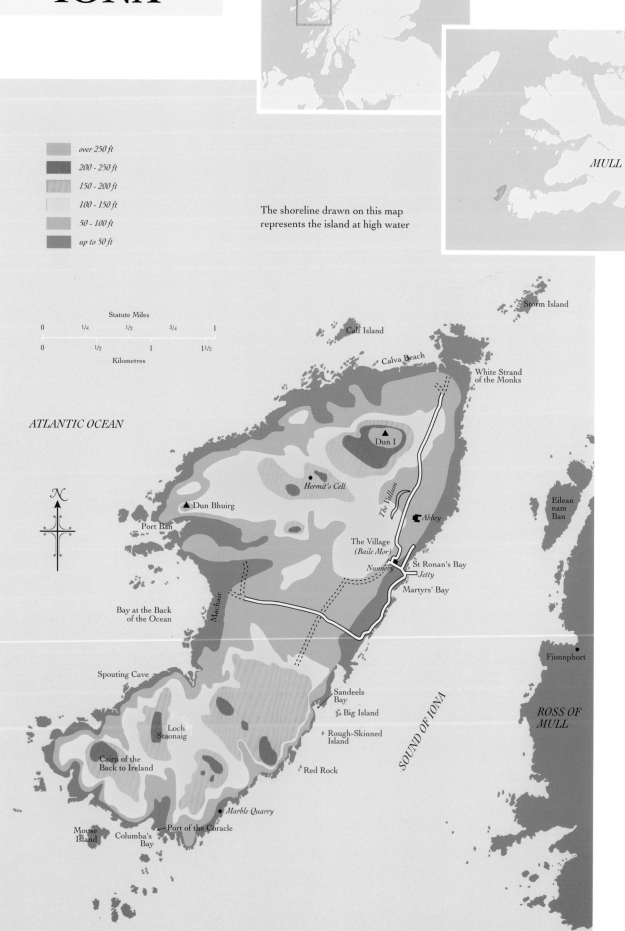

MULL

over 250 ft
200 - 250 ft
150 - 200 ft
100 - 150 ft
50 - 100 ft
up to 50 ft

The shoreline drawn on this map
represents the island at high water

Statute Miles

0   1/4   1/2   3/4   1

0   1/2   1   1½

Kilometres

ATLANTIC OCEAN

Storm Island

Calf Island

Calva Beach

White Strand
of the Monks

Dun I

Hermit's Cell

N

Dun Bhuirg

Port Ban

The Vallum

Abbey

Eilean
nam
Ban

The Village
(Baile Mor)

Nunnery

St Ronan's Bay

Jetty

Martyrs' Bay

Bay at the Back
of the Ocean

Machair

Fionnphort

Spouting Cave

Sandeels
Bay

Big Island

Rough-Skinned
Island

SOUND OF IONA

ROSS OF
MULL

Loch
Staonaig

Cairn of the
Back to Ireland

Red Rock

Marble Quarry

Mouse
Island

Columba's
Bay

Port of the Coracle

The 'holy island' of Iona came into the care of The National Trust for Scotland in 1979. Trust ownership, at the request of the Secretary of State for Scotland, was made possible by the generosity of the Hugh Fraser Foundation. The Foundation made available funds to buy the island from the Trustees of the 10th Duke of Argyll as a gift to the nation in memory of the late Lord Fraser of Allander, and provided the Trust with an endowment.

Iona is a small, fertile crofting island, of special significance to all Christians as the landing place of Columba and his followers, arriving from Ireland in AD 563.

The Trust has sought to recognise the role of each of the two communities on the island, the permanent population and that of the Abbey community, and has adopted a position of quiet support behind the scenes. It has tried to encourage conservation work on the island using volunteer work parties, known as Thistle Camps. These are made up predominantly of young people who spend a week or more doing tasks such as dyking, dune protection and other work to help the islanders.

Life on remote islands will always be difficult, with evidence of the harshness of the environment never far away. The deaths of the four islanders in a boating accident in December, 1998, during a routine crossing of the sound emphasised this to the wider world. The loss of these young men, who had decided to stay on the island and who thus embodied its hopes for the future, has been devastating for the island.

The Trust and others must now seek ways of helping the local community to rebuild their lives. I hope that all visitors to Iona will remember that island life is not always idyllic and that they will, in their own small way, contribute to the local economy and thus help the community towards a viable future.

Trevor Croft
Director, The National Trust for Scotland

SACRED
· ISLAND ·

1. EARLY DAYS ON IONA

Who were the first inhabitants of Iona? When did they come? How did they live? These questions are of interest to many people. Answers emerge only gradually, as the results of research by archaeologists and others become known: and those answers are necessarily hazy because they often have to be based on conflicting or inconclusive evidence, and because of our remoteness from those far-off days.

The first people to move into Scotland were Celts - hardy, red-haired, and with blue or green eyes. They gradually worked their way north through England. From about 4,500 BC they began occupying mainland Scotland, starting to colonise the Hebrides somewhat later, perhaps around 3,800 BC. These pioneers followed a hunter-gatherer, nomadic way of life.

Iona may not have appealed to these wandering folk who tended to migrate from place to place in family groups as the seasons rotated. The island might have seemed too restrictive. However Iona had important advantages: a short sea crossing from Mull, complete immunity from attacks by bears and wolves, level fertile land provided by the raised beaches, and a rocky shoreline which would regularly have yielded a harvest of shellfish. It is likely that there were some inhabitants on the island by 3,000 BC. In about 2,500 BC a more settled agricultural way of life began replacing the nomadic existence on Iona. There is secure evidence that farming communities had installed themselves there before 1,600 BC when, on the islands, the Neolithic age gave way to the Bronze age.

Until that time the ground was largely covered with hazel and birch. One version of the name of the Island translates into 'Island of Yews', so yews may also have thrived. Farming implies grazing which, over succeeding centuries, would have gradually prevented the regeneration of most of the trees.

In considering the security of its crops, its animals and its people, Iona's first requirement was to watch the waters to the west. For this reason the rocky hill Dun Bhuirg *(pronounced 'Dun Voo-rig')* near the western edge of Iona was turned into a protected look-out. It was backed by dwellings and other structures within a fortified perimeter. Deteriorating climate from around 1,000 BC reduced the area of

1. Inset above: Approaching Saint Columba's Bay

12

2. Dun Bhuirg seen from the east

4. The Hermit's Cell

*3. Dun I, Iona's isolated and
conspicuous hill*

productive land and thereby increased the value of what remained: much of this good land could be overseen from Dun Bhuirg. Interestingly, Dun I *(pronounced 'Dun EE')*, at 332 feet the island's highest top, twice the height of Dun Bhuirg and with commanding views all round, was apparently never fortified.

On Dun Bhuirg traces can still be seen today of the fort built there between 200 BC and 200 AD. Natural defence on the seaward face was provided by sheer cliff. On the other sides walls of about 10 feet thickness were constructed around a courtyard measuring 150 feet by 115 feet. Inside the sheltered space timber-framed huts were erected. Recent exploration within the site has unearthed remains of pottery made from Iona clay and the bones of cattle, sheep, pigs, and deer; and also beads dating from the first century.

An intriguing relic known as the Hermit's Cell lies between Dun Bhuirg and Dun I. It now consists of a 15-foot ring of undressed building stones standing on substantial foundations some three feet in width, with apparently provision for a door opening to the south-west, as was standard practice in early windowless dwellings in order to make full use of the afternoon daylight. Dry-stone walls against an adjacent rock face suggest enclosures for sheep or cattle. Conclusive information on the age of the Cell has not yet been found, though one school of thought asserts that it is as old as the Dun Bhuirg defences.

*5. A sandy cove close to
Dun Bhuirg, looking west*

There are no standing stones on Iona, but on the western portion of the Ross of Mull there are pre-Christian standing stones allegedly arranged in line as if to guide pilgrims and other travellers to the point of departure for Iona. The implication is that Iona was not simply inhabited but that the island was considered a place to be visited.

From about the year 300 the Highland Celts, united by a common hatred of the Roman army pressing them from the south, became known as Picts. In the fifth century travellers and traders from the Dalriada tribe based in the Antrim area of Northern Ireland paid increasingly frequent visits to the Argyll coast and its neighbouring islands. They started settling in Argyll. Rather confusingly, these incomers from Ireland were known as Scots. In about 500 AD the Dalriada ruling dynasty transferred its seat across the water to Dunadd, near Kilmartin in Argyll, regularising the existence of Scottish Dalriada.

6. *All that remains of the Dun Bhuirg fortifications*

Travel between islands, and between the mainland and islands, was generally accomplished more quickly and more safely by sea than by land. In this context Iona, far from being awkward to reach, would have been almost convenient, a hub for the sea-lanes of mariners. The island is only 75 miles from the north Antrim coast: the shortest crossing from Ireland to Scotland is just 20 miles.

Scholars differ in their views of the nature and extent of the pagan practices conducted on Iona before the arrival of Christianity, but it seems reasonable to believe that as elsewhere amongst the Hebrides druidic or other pre-Christian rituals, an amalgam of superstition and religion, were woven into the culture and were observed with commitment.

9. *The framework of a 25-foot replica coracle built in County Mayo and sailed from Antrim to Argyll in 1997 to mark the fourteenth centenary of St Columba's landing on Iona*

2. SAINT COLUMBA

7. Inset above: A detail from St Luke's Gospel in the Book of Kells - see page 20

On Sunday 9th June, 597, Saint Columba died on Iona at the age of 75 or 76. At a time when the lives of saints and other holy men spawned legend, and when written accounts were rare or non-existent, there has to be a fog of uncertainty shrouding almost every historical assertion. In contrast, the date attributed to Columba's death is widely taken as reliable: and his death was itself the climax of his astonishing life, guaranteeing his sainthood.

Traditionally, Columba is believed to have crossed from northern Ireland to reach Iona on Whitsun Eve 563. In the thirty-four years between setting foot on the island and his death Columba made Iona into a world-renowned centre of spiritual and cultural inspiration.

Columba was born about 521, of royal warrior stock, probably at Gartan in County Donegal, into what may have been a pagan environment. A century earlier Saint Patrick had begun converting influential leaders in Ireland to Christianity: by Columba's time there had been an expansion of the faith within both Ireland and parts of Scotland, and separately, though in a somewhat different form, Christianity was marching north through eastern England behind the Roman army.

In the period when Columba came to Iona there were frequent movements of traders, administrators, and other visitors crossing to and fro between the north of Ireland and the west coast of Scotland;

8. The pebbly beach at Columba's Bay

and once he had established himself and his community of monks on Iona Columba made several trips back to Ireland.

Columba's original voyage to Iona is usually said to have been made in a coracle, the use of that word being kept alive by the house journal of the current Iona Community which is called 'Coracle'. His vessel was, of course, very different from the tiny portable dinghies used by individual fishermen on rivers and estuaries in Wales and Ireland. Columba's sea-going coracle was of a long-favoured design for the boats which had been in daily use, in all weathers, for hundreds of years.

In Columba's day the frame of the coracle, or curragh, would have been made of a mesh of ash ribs and stringers, secured at the cross-over points with leather thongs. The spars and oars would also have been ash, selected from the tough north-facing sides of the trees. At that time tall ash flourished in Ireland away from the coast. The keel and gunwales would have been of oak. The whole structure would have been wrapped in animal hides stitched to one another with flax and sealed with wool grease and beeswax. Columba's craft would have been of this type and might well have been 50 or 60 or even 70 feet long. Forty years earlier Saint Brendan, the Irish abbot, made long voyages far out into the Atlantic in just such a coracle.

A sixth century coracle would have been light, drawing only a few inches when empty, but capable of transporting a load of several tons. It was designed and built entirely for peaceful activity, and was markedly different from the Viking longships described in Chapter 3.

In his coracle, accompanied by twelve supporters and no doubt an amount of food and luggage, Columba was supposed to have touched down on the south-east corner of Iona, in a bay now known as The Port of the Coracle; and once

10. A sketch showing the probable form of construction of sea-going coracles in the sixth century

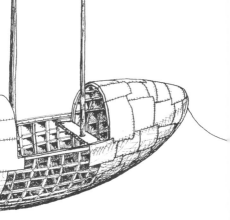

he had satisfied himself that Ireland was out of sight, he built a cairn on a knoll of high ground half a mile to the north-west called the Cairn of the Back to Ireland.

With his companions Columba erected his monastic church and dwellings, almost certainly building in timber, on the site of the current Abbey. Nothing of Columba's structures remains, though there are indications of a large number of post-holes. It is supposed that crosses were placed to mark sacred places on Iona, but they too would have been of wood and must long since have rotted away. What does remain is a major part of the mound and ditch, together called the vallum, which surrounded the original tract of about 20 acres on which the monastic foundation stood. The vallum can be seen most clearly behind the Abbey Coffee Shop, between it and the MacLeod Centre which stands a little way up the rising ground behind.

No contemporary account of Columba or his achievements exists, and we can only guess at his appearance though there seems every likelihood that he was hardy and physically strong. His voice it is said could be heard across the Sound of Iona on the Ross of Mull. There is a statue of him, indeed the only known statue of him, in a niche on the east face of the Bishop's House, a building mentioned further in Chapter 15: we do not know whether it is like him. Much legend, however, reinforced by writings from the eighth century and later, furnishes us with comprehensive, though sometimes conflicting, facts. The most notable contribution to the Columba story is Adomnan's *'Life of Saint Columba'* written about a hundred years after Columba's time on Iona. Adomnan was the ninth abbot of Iona, and was directly descended from Columba's paternal grandfather. His book gives enthralling detail of daily life on Iona in the sixth century, and provides records of

12. The statue of Saint Columba in a niche on the east wall of the Bishop's House

11. Part of the medieval mound and ditch, or vallum. This stretch to the north-west of the abbey runs close to the MacLeod Centre

15. The Book of Kells, folio 130 r.

The opening of St Marks' Gospel.

In the King James Authorised Version of the New Testament the words are: 'The beginning of the gospel of Jesus Christ, the Son of God.'

The latin form used in the Book of Kells is: 'Initium euangelii IHU XPI'.

A 12th century traveller, Giraldus Cambrensis, who studied the work, wrote of it:

'Fine craftsmanship is all about you, but you might not notice it. Look more keenly at it, and you will penetrate to the very shrine of art. You will make out intricacies, so delicate and subtle, so exact and compact, so full of knots and links, with colours so fresh and vivid, that you might say that all this was the work of an angel, and not of man.

'The oftener I see the book, and the more carefully I study it, the more I am lost in ever fresh amazement.'

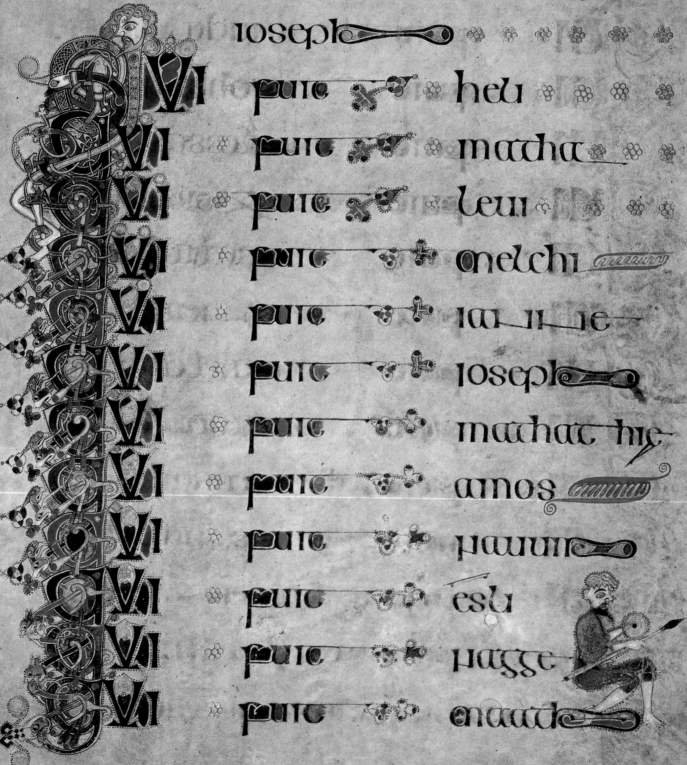

factus est uis filius meus dilectus in te

bene conplacuit mihi ·

Ipse ihs erat incipiens quasi an

horum triginta ut putabatur filius

ioseph

qui fuit heli

qui fuit matha

qui fuit leui

qui fuit melchi

qui fuit ianne

qui fuit ioseph

qui fuit mathat hie

qui fuit amos

qui fuit nauum

qui fuit esli

qui fuit nagge

qui fuit maath

200

miracles performed by Columba; but it is tantalisingly short of conventional biographical detail.

The picture of Columba that comes down to us across the ages is of a vastly energetic leader, with tremendous religious zeal and personal magnetism, coupled with extraordinary craft skill and administrative ability. He also wrote hymns and is credited with transcribing 300 books with his own hand. Claims are made that he was a supremely talented illuminator of sacred documents. Whether or not he personally contributed to the Book of Kells will probably never be known, but we can be sure that the reputation for excellence which he fostered would have animated work on that wonderful manuscript.

The Book of Kells is a lavishly decorated collection of the four gospels, in Latin, mainly stemming from Saint Jerome's Vulgate text of the late fourth century. It consists of elegant, steady, bold text, enriched with exceedingly elaborate illumination, executed with great skill and subtlety, employing colours that have barely faded in almost 1,500 years. When we allow for the nature of the pens and brushes likely to have been available, and the quality of the lighting in which work was carried out, the result is utterly magical. That the Book was started on Iona is practically certain: that it was completely produced on the island is just possible. Certainly, finished or not, the Book of Kells was on Iona when the Vikings came.

From the first, Columba appears to have lost no time in expounding the gospel and in recruiting novices. Iona became under his energetic leadership a renowned centre for the training of monks.

Columba was quick to renew his contact with Conall, the King of Scottish Dalriada. He also trekked up the Great Glen to make his peace with the pagan Pictish ruler, King Bridei, at Inverness, and succeeded in impressing him and possibly even converting him to Christianity. Bridei gave his blessing to missionary efforts by Columba as far east as Tayside.

All this activity was on top of the need for Columba to supervise and encourage the numerous monastic daughter houses that he had set up in the Hebrides and in Ireland. Those in Ireland included the famous foundation at Durrow. On mainland

15. St Martin's Cross seen from the east

14. The Book of Kells, folio 200 r.

The beginning of the genealogy of Christ from St Luke's Gospel, Chapter 3, verses 23 onwards. The latin equivalents of the names in the King James Authorised Version of the New Testament, namely Joseph, Heli, Matthat, Levi, Melchi..., can be recognised.

16. Some of the 600-strong gathering of Roman Catholics commemorating the thirteenth centenery of Saint Columba's death

Scotland he concentrated on winning over the Pictish clans to the north and west of the Grampians. All these endeavours appear to have been fruitful. Christianity spread vigorously, but benignly, outwards from Iona.

Columba also increasingly fastened his eye on Northumbria and eastern Scotland. Although he may not have visited those areas himself it was not many years before teams from Iona took the Columban message to them, and by the middle of the seventh century there were probably Columban foundations in Fife, Atholl, and Easter Ross; and there was contact with the religious leaders in Northumberland. All the while Iona was increasing its influence and its reputation as a powerful centre of the Christian faith.

17. The steamer PS 'Grenadier' operated by David MacBrayne out of Oban

22

The esteem in which Saint Columba is held can be gauged by the enthusiasm with which very large numbers of people attend occasions staged in his honour. In 1897, on 9th June, dignitaries and clergy, prominent laymen, pilgrims, and visitors from every imaginable place gathered on Iona to commemorate the thirteenth centenary of the death of Columba. The Abbey Church had a temporary roof, allowing divine service to be held there: the first Gaelic service in the Abbey since the Reformation. The day was brilliantly warm and sunny, and the sea was calm. The throng strolling on the grass outside the Abbey in their late-Victorian finery must have made an engaging sight. After four hours on the island everyone was taken back to Oban by the David MacBrayne steamer Grenadier. A few days later, at the invitation of the Duke of Argyll, 600 Roman Catholics visited Iona for the same purpose.

On the first Sunday in June, 1963, a huge crowd of all denominations assembled on Iona to mark the fourteenth centenary of Columba's arrival on Iona, by hearing an open-air address by Lord MacLeod.

And the 9th June, 1997, the fourteenth centenary of Columba's death, was commemorated on Iona and in surrounding areas in many ways, by services and other events throughout the year, and by special publications. A banner to mark the occasion was brought from the parish of Llanfairisgaer in North Wales, and presented in the Abbey where it is on display. A highlight of the centenary celebrations was provided by Mary Robinson, President of the Republic of Ireland, who opened the new permanent Saint Columba Welcome and Iona Abbey Information Point at Fionnphort directly opposite Iona across the Sound.

18. The Llanfairisgaer banner carried from North Wales to Iona Abbey in 1997 for the forteenth centenary of Saint Columba's death. The stylised goose is an ancient symbol for the Holy Spirit, and as 'The Wild Goose' it is now the logo of the Iona Community's publishing business

The monastic life of the foundation on Iona, and the bloodless evangelism forging its way across Scotland and into north-east England, proceeded under the sequence of abbots who followed Saint Columba throughout the seventh and most of the eighth centuries; and would probably have continued to do so for succeeding decades or even centuries were it not for stirrings to the north.

3. VIKING RAIDS

Sometime after about 750 the area now made up of Denmark, Norway, and Sweden developed a vigorous and expanding appetite for additional farm land and for supplementary sources of wealth. The combined population, thought to have been at that time about two million, united by a common language, was prompted by a sustained growth in numbers, a huge expansion of the Scandinavian iron industry, and the new opportunities for taking prizes offered by increasing maritime trading traffic, to host a culture of authorised piracy. The pirates were known collectively as Vikings. The reputation of Vikings for violence, cruelty, and stamina has remained intact ever since.

The Vikings would not have been a threat had it not been for their superb seamanship. The Viking longship, which had been continuously refined over a lengthy period had, by say the year 775, become a fast, robust, ocean-going craft. Furthermore the longship was revered by the whole people: an invitation to join the crew of a longship had become an honour. All men making up the complement were skilled with both oar and sword.

Our knowledge of the structure of Viking longships is soundly based because of the large number that have by good fortune survived, albeit in various degrees of dilapidation. Of these vessels the most complete is the Gokstad ship dating from about the year 850 on display in the Viking Ship Hall in Oslo. This longship was of medium size, with 16 oars each side. A crew of 50 might have been carried to provide for reliefs. There would also have been room for 20 or 30 prisoners or extra soldiers. She was about 76 feet in overall length, 17 feet 6 inches in beam, and almost 6 feet 6 inches from gunwale to keel amidships; and when afloat would have drawn no more than 2 feet 6 inches unladen. Such vessels were decked at a level which

20. Sketch of a small Viking longship

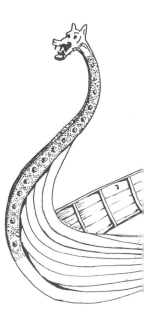

19. Inset above: A sandy beach on the north shore of Iona

21. Part of the White Strand of the Monks with the Storm Island tombolo in the middle distance

22. Grotesque head on the prow of a Viking longship

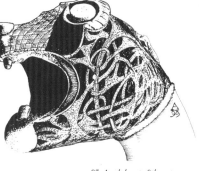

23. An elaborate 9th century Viking figure-head

allowed the rowers to operate in comfort and with efficiency, while providing sheltered space for stores and off-duty crewmen. The largest longships may have been about 100 feet in length, with perhaps thirty oars on each side.

The longship was propelled principally by oarsmen helped, should there be a following wind, by the single square sail. The vessel was fast: in 1892 a replica with a Norwegian crew crossed the Atlantic in four weeks. Each Viking ship was clinker-built with oak strakes held to the oak frame with hard-wood pegs called tree-nails. There was little if any metal. Internal fastenings were made with ties from the inner bark of lime trees, known as bask. Caulking consisted of animal hair made into strings. This form of construction gave the longship elasticity and resilience, allowing it to yield to the impact of heavy seas and immediately recover from temporary distortion. Steering was by a broad paddle rigged over the starboard (steer-board) quarter. The oars, made of spruce, were elegantly shaped, and graded so that longer ones were used towards the stem and the stern. They passed through circular holes in the uppermost strakes. Protection above the gunwale was afforded to the crew by shields rigged vertically on each side of the vessel.

The exaggerated prow was often elegantly carved, and usually topped with a grotesque head calculated to terrify enemies. A fleet of these vessels, sometimes consisting of up to 200 longships, presented the Vikings with a formidable fighting machine: there is one report of 400 such vessels assailing English, French, and Russian coasts. Raiding parties sallied from their Scandinavian bases to attack the Scottish Islands, the east coast of England and up the Thames estuary, and at times much further afield. Because of the shallow draught they were able to reach Paris and attack the city successfully. Viking fleets followed the Biscay coast and entered the Mediterranean. The passage to Iona would have been a short-haul voyage.

The main goal of the Vikings was consistent: namely to plunder gold, silver and jewellery; to take healthy prisoners who could be sold as slaves; and to capture nobles for whom ransom could be demanded. To make their belligerent descents on coastal areas as productive as possible, Vikings resorted to deliberate violence, resulting in deaths amongst the local inhabitants, as a way of generating fear and confusion. Settlement was always secondary and was only pursued once the invaders had made several successive incursions and had ensured that a piece of violated territory would be suitable for their families and for agricultural development.

The Vikings first descended on Britain in the year 789, near

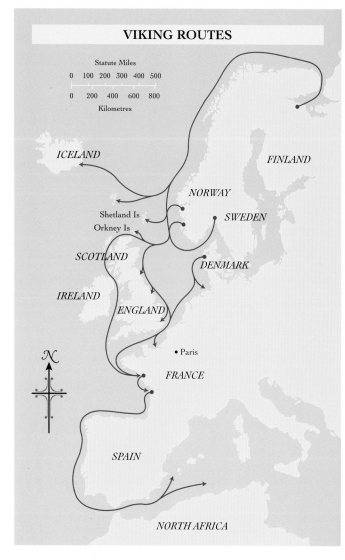

VIKING ROUTES

Statute Miles

0 100 200 300 400 500

0 200 400 600 800
Kilometres

ICELAND

FINLAND

NORWAY

SWEDEN

Shetland Is
Orkney Is

SCOTLAND

DENMARK

IRELAND

ENGLAND

Paris

FRANCE

SPAIN

NORTH AFRICA

Dorchester. In 793 they attacked Lindisfarne, destroying sacred buildings, killing many monks, and slaughtering the cattle. Soon it was the turn of Iona. The first Viking raid on the island was in 795. The next in 802, the invaders wreaking terrible damage; and then in 806 they came again, massacring 68 monks at Martyrs' Bay. The following year the Abbot of Iona decamped to the infant foundation at the relatively secure site at Kells, thirty-five miles north-west of Dublin, where most of the remaining monks from Iona went. There was said to have been yet another Viking raid on Iona when two monks of the small religious community that had stayed on the island were murdered on the north-east shore at a scenic spot known as the White Strand of the Monks. Some sources declare that Vikings made six separate raids on Iona, although once the wealth of monastic sites was known to have been exhausted the motivation for further raids would have evaporated.

In 807 The Book of Kells was taken from Iona to Kells for safekeeping. It can be seen today in Trinity College, Dublin.

The Vikings appear to have decided against colonising Iona. In contrast, they apparently looked favourably upon Mull: many of the place names on the western half of Mull are of Norse origin. The Vikings settled on the Shetland Islands, which remained Norwegian for six hundred years, the Orkney Islands, Caithness, and a over a wide band across central England.

After some 300 years of predation the buccaneering reign of the Vikings was brought to a close by King Harold of England, who won a decisive victory over Harald 'Hardraade', King of Norway, at Stamford Bridge, a few miles east of York, in September 1066.

24. A watercolour by Tom Shanks of the White Strand of the Monks, showing Storm Island, with the hills of Mull in the background

4. THE BENEDICTINE ABBEY

By the middle of the 12th century all the people of the islands of the Hebrides, and the mainland west of the Great Glen as far north as Ullapool, had started to see themselves as an entity to be known later as the Lordship of the Isles: from 1156 this composite area was controlled by Somerled, a Clan Donald chieftain who was half Norse, half Celt, and who had defeated the local Norse rulers. Somerled died in 1164, and was succeeded by his son Reginald.

Despite the departure of most of the Iona monks to Kells in Ireland in 807, a depleted monastic community still following the Irish devotional practices brought by Columba, survived on Iona into the late 12th century. Around this time Reginald allowed the Benedictine order to establish a foundation on Iona. They built their abbey on the site that Saint Columba had used, modelling it on other Benedictine houses in western Europe, creating by far the largest and most elaborate ecclesiastical structure in the west Highlands.

The Benedictine order sprang from the spiritual life adopted by Saint Benedict who was born near Perugia in Italy in the year 480. He promulgated his 'Rule' in 526. In his ideal community there would be self-sufficiency, with members needing no contacts outside the monastery, spending four hours a day on prayer, four on spiritual reading, and up to six on manual work. The earliest recorded introduction of the Rule in Britain was towards the end of the seventh century. Benedictism flowered here in the eighth century, only to wither abruptly in the ninth in the face of Viking assaults. After a pause of some decades, following the Norman Conquest of England, the Benedictines re-established themselves in Britain, building 34 monasteries across the land.

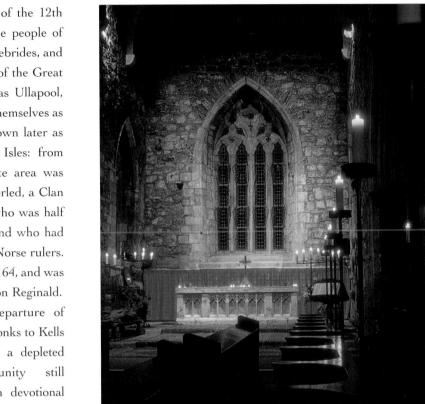

28. *The chancel and east window of the Abbey*

27. *Intricate carving on a medieval grave cover. Note the galley which was a popular design on stonework in the Hebrides*

30. The doorway of St. Oran's Chapel, built in the 12th century

The regime of life under the Rule was hard, with severe discipline and rigidly imposed schedules of divine services several times each day and night; and programmes of work, prescribed diets, and silence. Much of the work consisted of heavy agricultural labouring, cultivating and bringing in potatoes, oats, flax, and from time to time other crops. This effort would have been expended both inside the vallum and in areas further afield. There would also have been some horticultural tasks that would have been less physically demanding such as growing herbs to be used as cures and for adding interest to meals. These herbs, grown successfully at the Abbey now, would have done well in earlier centuries and so probably would have made up the inventory of the medieval Iona herb-garden:

Artichoke	Oregano
Borage	Rue
Bowles Mint	Sage
Comfrey	St John's Wort
Fennel	Sorrel
Feverfew	Tansy
Lemonbalm	Tarragon
Mint	

The earliest surviving stone building in the Abbey complex is Saint Oran's Chapel which may date from about 1180. Its associated burial ground, the Reilig Odhrain *(pronounced 'Reel ig Oran')*, may be even older. A plot dedicated as a graveyard would have been an important feature of the previous monastic site, though it may also have been used as a lay burial ground. There were many Christian memorials in the Reilig Odhrain. A recent survey listed 10 crosses, 11 effigies, and 150 grave covers and grave slabs. Some of these historic items are

29. The remains of the internal wall which ran across the old Bishop's House, north of the abbey

31. MacLean's Cross

32. Wonderful carving on the broken shaft of a medieval cross

33. Effigies of uniformed figures on grave slabs

now in the Abbey museum and a few in the cloister. The oldest of the monuments were probably carved in the 12th century. There is no direct evidence of the alleged earlier burial of Scottish, Norwegian, and Irish kings, although there has long been a belief that 40 or more do lie under the turf surrounding the abbey.

The paved path which connects the Abbey Church to the Reilig Odhrain, known as 'The Road of the Dead', is the finest medieval road in Europe. It used to extend to Martyrs' Bay where coffins brought from the mainland were taken ashore until less than a hundred years ago.

The Abbey buildings, and particularly the Abbey Church itself, begun in about 1200, enjoyed successive phases of extension and refinement throughout the 13th century, and again in the 15th century. The builders and masons acquired the stone from three main sources: sandstone for plinths, lintels, and buttresses came from Carsaig on the south shore of the Ross of Mull; red granite for walls came from the island of Eilean nam Ban in Iona Sound and from around Torr Mor on the extreme western edge of the Ross of Mull; and grey or black siliceous rock for flagstones from quarries on Iona.

In 1493 the Benedictines' right to the Abbey was forfeited to the Crown, and the Abbey lost its independent status passing into the possession of the Bishops of the Isles, who made Iona Abbey Church their official seat and accorded it the title of 'Cathedral'. The word Cathedral has been used informally since the Reformation.

34. St. John's Cross, looking north-west

The free-standing crosses near the Abbey Church, and in the museum, are outstanding medieval creations. The ring cross is typical of the Celtic form, the ring providing both structural strength and symbolic significance: the circle implies eternity and equality, and suggests the presence of a halo. These crosses, sometimes called 'high crosses', are carved with spiral and other ornament and with biblical characters and animals, all executed with astonishing precision.

Saint Martin's Cross by the west front of the Abbey Church has stood undisturbed and undamaged on its plinth of pink granite since the eighth century. Saint John's Cross nearby, a dramatic structure with a wide span, is a replica of the original eighth century cross which shattered in an accident: the original has been imaginatively reconstructed and placed in the Abbey museum. MacLean's Cross is rather later, dating from the last years of the Benedictine presence, exhibiting delicate interlacing and foliage despite damage to the arms: on its west-facing side there is a deeply incised crucifixion scene. The cross stands on the bend in the road just east of the parish church.

36. St Martin's Cross,
looking west

There is legend that 360 high crosses once stood on Iona and that all but a handful were broken and thrown into the sea at the time of the Reformation. The legend is suspect because no fragments of such crosses have been found and the crosses would, in any case, have been too heavy to shift without co-ordinated effort: the yarn is more likely to have been spun as anti-protestant propaganda.

A small steep-roofed attachment to the west wall of the Abbey Church is known as Saint Columba's Shrine. It may stand over a spot where Columba prayed, but probably it never housed his bones. In the middle ages the whereabouts of the physical remains of saints was a matter of acute interest, and the monks took enormous care to conceal those of Columba. Legend has it that his remains were divided between Dunkeld and a site in Ireland. The richly-jewelled Monymusk reliquary was also supposed to hold Saint Columba's bones and in that belief Robert the Bruce usually carried it into battle, and it is known

37. Sedilia in the south wall of the abbey sanctuary,
behind the effigy of Abbot Dominic, who died in 1465

35. St Martin's Cross,
looking east

58. One of the decorative capitals on the columns between the Choir and the south aisle of the Abbey Church

that he had it with him at Bannockburn. The reliquary is now on show in the New Museum of Scotland: but what really became of Saint Columba will probably never be known.

Although the Abbey Church was substantially built, only a little of the stonework we see today dates from the 13th and 14th centuries. For example, part of the north wall of the choir is 13th century while the rest belongs to the late 15th century, as does the tower. Most of the nave is 15th century or newer. Nonetheless there are many examples of interesting, intricate, stone carving of the medieval period to be seen in the Abbey Church and in the cloister. Some of the column capitals, and the sedilia, which date from the 15th century, are worth inspecting. The cloister dates from the 13th century, with two of its original paired columns still in position.

One effect of the withdrawal of patronage from the Abbey in 1493 was the dispersal of the craftsmen who had been working there. The religious life continued until about 1560 when the Scottish Reformation reached Iona bringing its monastic phase quietly to a close. The influence of John Knox may have helped to secure the relative tranquillity of this phase in Iona's story. Thereafter the Abbey buildings stood silent, falling gradually into disrepair. Fortunately the ruins were not extensively ransacked for the stone but the roof timbers seem to have soon disappeared.

40. Overleaf: The array of windows over the west door of the Abbey Church

39. The abbey cloister forming a square, with the Lipchitz sculpture depicting the descending holy dove

At the time that the Benedictines were starting to build their abbey on Iona the Augustinian order were also at work, building their Nunnery 300 yards to the south. There was no rivalry between those responsible for these two enterprises, despite the coincidence of the timing. The Benedictines were making a measured expansion of their monastic endeavour throughout Britain: the Augustinians, enthusiasts for nunneries to the exclusion of monasteries, selected Iona for their second foundation in Scotland having already positioned their first at Perth. By the 13th century there were many Augustinian nunneries in Ireland, so expansion into Scotland would have seemed rational. In choosing Iona both orders must have been impressed with the island's stature as a centre of spirituality, culture, and learning.

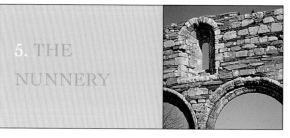

5. THE NUNNERY

41. Inset above: Nunnery Church wall

43. The west wall of the Nunnery Church

42. Watercolour of the Nunnery ruins by Pat Malpas, 1997

The early Christian church recognised two saints called Augustine. The more recent, who was Italian, and who was sent by the pope in 596 to convert the Anglo-Saxons in Britain and who became the first Archbishop of Canterbury, did not give his name to the Augustinians. Rather, it was Augustine of Hippo. He lived from 354 to 430, for most of the time in north Africa. He was a prodigious author, writing a monumental work of 22 books representing human history in terms of the conflict between the spiritual and the temporal.

Although Reginald had gladly given his blessing to both the Abbey and the Nunnery projects, he tied

44. A late Victorian photograph of the derelict Nunnery Church

*45. A careful 18th century drawing of the Nunnery Church,
before the archways were filled in and the foliage removed*

himself closely to the nunnery by appointing his sister to be the first prioress. The inmates of the Nunnery were termed canonesses, coming from clergy families and from wealthy backgrounds. Little has been told of numbers at the Nunnery, or of how they fared.

46. A recent photograph from a viewpoint close to that used for the illustration on page 38

Unlike the Abbey, most of the 13th century stonework, which includes the whole of the Nunnery church, has survived well and much is still clearly visible. The architectural style is based on Irish practice, such as the positioning of the clerestory windows over columns instead of over arches, so as to allow a lower roof-line without loss of light. The presence of an original cloister about 45-foot square can be deduced, but not seen. The 15th century modifications included an enlargement of the cloister of which surviving fragments indicate that there were finely carved arches and other decoration.

47. The building at the south side of the cloister which would probably have been the Nunnery refectory

To the north of the main Nunnery buildings stands the detached Church of St Ronan, now a museum of medieval sculpture. The church was probably built at the same time as the Nunnery, though it was originally the parish church for Iona. Below the floor evidence has been found suggesting the existence of an earlier, smaller structure which may also have been used by the lay population, and earlier still there appears to have been a burial ground on the same site.

As with the Abbey the monastic life of the Nunnery ran out in the middle of the 16th century. The last abbess died in 1543. Today the ruins form a picturesque reminder of the Augustinian period, enhanced in the 1920s by the garden which now lies in the Nunnery precinct.

48. An aerial view of the Nunnery with St. Ronan's Church on the right and the refectory on the left

49. Stonework on the inside of the south wall of the Nunnery Church

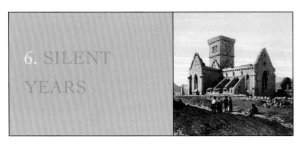

6. SILENT YEARS

From about 1560 until 1899 the Abbey and the Nunnery slid gradually but continuously towards decrepitude. Roofs gave way, stonework crumbled, doors collapsed, and sheep and cattle moved in to shelter from the weather. During this interval numerous events which were of importance to the residents of the island occurred, as we shall see in later chapters; but monastically these were the silent years.

Many interesting accounts of visits to Iona were recorded by travellers to the island during this time. Here is a selection.

Martin Martin

Martin Martin, the energetic Scottish explorer and author, went to Iona towards the close of the 17th century. These extracts from his report on the island give the flavour of his thoroughness, though perhaps we may not always extol his accuracy:

'This isle in the Irish Language is called I. Colmkil, i.e. the isthmus of Columbus the clergyman. Colum was his proper name, and the addition of kil, which signifies a church, was added by the islanders by way of excellence.

'The isle is two miles long from south to north, and one in breadth, from east to west. The east side is all arable and plain, fruitful in corn and grass; the west side is high and rocky.

'This isle was anciently a seminary of learning, famous

50. Inset above: An early view of the derelict Abbey Church, from the south-east

for the severe discipline and sanctity of Columbus. He built two churches and two monasteries in it, one for men, the other for women, which were endowed by the Kings of Scotland and of the Isles. Near Saint Columba's tomb is Saint Martin's cross, an entire stone of eight feet high; it is a very hard and red stone, with a mixture of grey in it.

52. The Abbey photographed from the south-west in about 1880. The roofless walls of St. Oran's Chapel, and the Reilig Odhrain, are in the foreground

'On the south side of the church, mentioned above, is the burial-place in which the kings and chiefs of the tribes are buried, and over them a shrine: there was an inscription, giving an account of each particular tomb, but time has worn them off. The middlemost had written on it "The Tombs of the Kings of Scotland" of which forty-eight lie there.'

51. A detail from the map of the west coast of Scotland, drawn in 1610 by John Speed (see page115), showing the area around Iona. Mull is written as 'Mu...la' and Iona as 'Colmkil or Iona Ile'.

Dr Samuel Johnson and James Boswell landed on Iona on 19th October, 1773, clutching a copy of Martin Martin's book: they stayed overnight in a barn on the island, returning to Mull the following day. Both wrote about this visit, but here we draw only on Johnson. The last two sentences of the first paragraph of this extract are possibly the best known words ever written about Iona, and are also amongst Johnson's most quotable sayings.

'At last we came to Icolmkill, but found no convenience for landing. Our boat could not be forced very near the dry ground, and our Highlanders carried us over the water. We were now treading that illustrious Island, which was once the luminary of the Caledonian regions, whence savage clans and roving barbarians derived the benefits of knowledge, and the

Dr Samuel Johnson and James Boswell

blessings of religion... That man is little
to be envied, whose patriotism would
not gain force upon the plain of
Marathon, or whose piety would
not grow warmer among the
ruins of Iona!

'The chapel of the nunnery is
now used by the inhabitants as a
kind of general cow-house, and
the bottom is consequently too
miry for examination. Some of the
stones which covered the later
abbesses have inscriptions, which might
yet be read, if the chapel were cleansed. The
roof of this, as of all other buildings, is totally
destroyed, not only because timber quickly decays,
but because in an island utterly destitute of wood, it was wanted
for use, and was consequently the first plunder of needy rapacity.

55. Portrait of Dr Samuel
Johnson engraved in 1785

'A large space of ground about these consecrated edifices is covered
with gravestones, few of which have any inscription. He that surveys
it, attended by an insular antiquary, may be told where the kings of
many nations are buried, and if he loves to sooth
his imagination with the thoughts that naturally
rise in places where the great and the powerful lie
mingled with the dust, let him listen in submissive
silence; for if he asks any questions, his delight is
at an end. By whom the subterraneous vaults are
peopled is now utterly unknown. The graves are
very numerous, and some of them undoubtedly
contain the remains of men, who did not expect to
be so soon forgotten.

'It is observed, that ecclesiastical colleges
are always in the most pleasant and fruitful
places. While the world allows the monks their
choice, it is surely no dishonour that they chose
well. This Island is remarkably fruitful. The
village near the churches is said to contain
seventy families, which, at five to a family, is

54. James Boswell, 31 years younger than
Johnson, seen here in about 1790, from an
engraving by John Jones

more than a hundred inhabitants to a mile. There are perhaps other villages; yet both corn and cattle are annually exported.

'But the fruitfulness of Iona is now its whole prosperity. The inhabitants are remarkably gross, and remarkably neglected: I know not if they are visited by any minister. The Island, which was once the metropolis of learning and piety, has now no school for education and only two of the inhabitants that can speak English, and not one that can write or read.

'We now left those illustrious ruins, by which Mr Boswell was much affected, nor would I willingly be thought to have looked on them without some emotion. Perhaps, in the revolutions of the world, Iona may be sometime again the instructress of the Western Regions.'

Johnson might be using colourful language to simplify a hard problem when he said 'by whom the subterraneous vaults are now peopled is utterly unknown'; but he probably did know that in Macbeth (*Act 2, Scene IV*) Shakespeare makes Ross ask MacDuff 'Where is Duncan's body?'. MacDuff replies 'Carried to Colmekill, the sacred storehouse of his predecessors and guardian of their bones'. Duncan was King of Scotland from 1034 till 1040: Colmekill was one of many spellings of Iona in the middle ages.

Sir Walter Scott, Scottish novelist, poet, lawyer, civic dignitary and statesman, made visits to Iona in 1810 and again in 1814.

Scott refers to his first trip to Iona, when he was a guest on the Isle of Ulva on the west side of Mull, in several letters. This paragraph is from a letter to Lady Abercorn written shortly after seeing Iona for the first time:

'The proprietor of the isle (of Ulva) Macdonald of Staffa a fine high-spirited young Chieftain was our pilot and guide through the Hebrides. He is much loved by his people whose prosperity he studies very much.

'I wish I could say so of the Duke of Argyle but his isles are in a wretched state. That of Iona in particular, where it is said Christianity

55. An early image of the Abbey Church with a gable-end of the cap room on top of the tower still in position. The ruin of Michael Chapel, on its diverging alignment, is in the foreground

56. Sir Walter Scott's portrait by Sir Henry Raeburn painted in 1822 when Scott was aged 51

Sir Walter Scott

57. A photograph from about 1890 showing the pathway up to the village from the jetty, with children at their stall trying to sell Iona pebbles to visitors

was first planted in Scotland and which still exhibits many curious and even splendid remains of monastic grandeur, is now in a most deplorable condition. The inhabitants are so numerous in proportion to the size of the island that (although it is a fertile spot comparing it with the other isles around it) it is barely sufficient to support them in the most wretched state possible in ordinary years - in those of scarcity they must starve for they have nothing to pay for imported corn - Much of this misery might I apprehend be remedied by a well regulated encouragement to fishermen for the sea abounds with fish of every description. But such a system to prevent peculation and abuse must be carried on under the countenance of an active benevolent, and at the same time resolute landlord. We were surrounded on the beach by boys and girls almost naked all begging for charity and offering pebbles for sale.'

In fairness to John Campbell, who was the Fifth Duke of Argyll from 1770 to 1806, it is known that as landlord of vast estates which included Iona he initiated imaginative land reforms which brought real benefits to his tenants.

Of the second visit, on 27th and 28th August, 1814, Scott was a guest on board the yacht 'Pharos' belonging to the Commissioners for Northern Lights. With the Commissioners he had just been, on a foul day, to inspect the exposed reef 10 miles south-west of Tiree called Skerryvore for which a lighthouse was being proposed. Happy to have survived that ordeal, he wrote:

58. Effigies of kings or noblemen on grave covers in the Reilig Odhrain before they were taken to the museum

'Came on board proud of our achievement; and, to the great delight of all parties, put the ship before the wind, and run swimmingly down for Iona. We soon got on shore, and landed in the bay of Martyrs, beautiful for its white sandy beach. Here all dead bodies are still landed, and laid for a time upon a small rocky eminence, called the Sweyne, before they are interred.

'Iona, the last time I saw it, seemed to me to contain the most wretched people I had anywhere seen. But either they have got better since I was here, or my eyes, familiarised with wretchedness of Zetland and the Harris, are less shocked with that of Iona. Certainly their houses are better than either, and the appearance of the people is not worse. This little fertile island contains upward of 400 inhabitants, all living upon small farms, which they divide and subdivide as their families increase, so that the country is greatly over-peopled, and in some danger of a famine in case of a year of scarcity.'

59. A miniature of John Keats by his friend Joseph Severn, painted within a year or two of Keats' visit to Iona

John Keats

John Keats spent a few hours on Iona on 24th July, 1818. In a letter to his youngest brother Tom, who died that year aged 19, Keats described his 'most wretched walk' from Grasspoint in south-east Mull, where he disembarked after crossing from Oban, to Fionnphort which he reached two days later. He related how, on Iona, the schoolmaster had showed him the ruins and the graveyard where, it was said, that 61 kings lay buried; and had given him the story of Saint Columba. All these particulars, and an account of 'the most interesting antiquities', were relayed home in this letter. There is a suspicion, however, that his interest was ready to be diverted to Staffa which he went on to visit later the same day and which did, indeed, make a profound impression on him.

Felix Mendelssohn

Felix Mendelssohn, in his diary for 8th August, 1829, wrote:

'Iona, one of the Hebrides-sisters - there is truly a very Ossianic and sweetly sad sound about that name - when in some future time I shall sit in a madly crowded assembly with music and dancing round me, and the wish arises to retire into the loneliest loneliness, I shall think of Iona with its ruins of a once magnificent cathedral, the remains of a convent, the graves of ancient Scotch Kings and still more ancient pirate-princes - with their ships rudely carved on many a monumental stone. If I had my home on Iona, and lived there upon melancholy as other people do on their rents, my darkest moment would be when in that wide space, that deals with nothing but cliffs and sea-gulls, suddenly a curl of steam should appear, followed by a ship and finally a gay party in veils and frock coats, who would look for an hour at the ruins and graves and the three little huts for the living, and then move off again.'

60. Felix Mendelssohn. A lithograph from 1830 when he was 21

Queen Victoria

Queen Victoria, in the Royal Yacht, dropped anchor off Iona on 19th August, 1847. Coming directly from Staffa where she had been rowed into Fingal's Cave, which greatly impressed her and

which she described in her journal in her usual exuberant prose, she limited herself to this rather restrained entry about Iona:

'Albert and Charles landed and were absent an hour. I and the ladies sketched. We saw from the yacht the ruins of the old cathedral of St Oran. When Albert and Charles returned, they said the ruins were very curious, there had been two monasteries there, and fine old crosses and tombs of ancient kings were to be seen. I must see it some time.'

If we remember that in 1847 the islanders were close to starvation, and highly apprehensive of their future, because of the devastating potato blight which reached its dreadful worst the previous year, we are reminded of how remote, both physically and emotionally, London then was from the Highlands and Islands, and how those in the south seemed incapable of responding to the acute problems faced by those in the north.

Taken together, these passages arm the reader with a strong impression of how Iona struck educated, travelled, visitors in the silent years.

There are quotations from many other travellers to Iona in *'That Illustrious Island ...Iona through Travellers' Eyes'* by E Mairi MacArthur and in *'Historic Visitors to Mull, Iona & Staffa'* by Eve Eckstein.

*61. William Daniell's 1815 aquatint
'Iona from the north-east'*

The strength of the Campbells, led by the Earls and later by the Dukes of Argyll, and the extent of their holdings of land, grew throughout the 16th and 17th centuries. A stage in the process was to obtain control of the whole of Iona in about 1690. The Dukes of Argyll then held Iona for over 200 years.

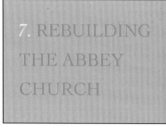

7. REBUILDING THE ABBEY CHURCH

62. The silver cross found by Lord MacLeod, installed on the Abbey Church communion table

The Eighth Duke and his architect Sir Robert Anderson began to make repairs to the Abbey Church in the 1870s, but soon decided to make a gift of the Abbey buildings, the Reilig Odhrain, and the Nunnery ruins, to a trust to look after them in perpetuity. The trustees were the Moderator of the General Assembly of the Church of Scotland and two other officials of the Church, the leaders of the established church in Edinburgh and Glasgow Cathedrals, and the principals of the four ancient Scottish universities. They were called collectively the Iona Cathedral Trustees.

The terms of the trust deed, dated 1899, provided for the restored Abbey Church to be made available for use by all Christian denominations, and that restoration was to begin as soon as funds allowed. The appearance of the Abbey Church was

64. Opposite page: The rebuilt chancel as it appears today

63. A photograph taken in 1875 of the south side of the chancel and the south transept shortly before the Duke of Argyll took the first steps in restoring the Abbey Church

to follow as closely as practicable that of the 15th century building. The book *'Columba's Island'* by E Mairi MacArthur contains detail of this historic arrangement. The Duke died in 1900, before work began; but he had nonetheless provided for the future reconstruction and preservation of the religious structures of Iona. The Abbey Church was rebuilt between 1902 and 1910.

Thereafter enhancements were introduced from time to time. The spectacular altar made of Iona marble, and the font with its stand of Iona marble, were installed. The important Justice Carpet covering much of the chancel floor was added; and many minor refinements were made. A programme of rolling maintenance was introduced.

66. Sunrise reflected in the east window of the Abbey Church south aisle chapel

65. The magnificent Abbey Church communion table, made of Iona marble, and the Justice Carpet

67. The wooden roof over the chancel

The Duke had expressed a wish for the unusual cap room that was placed on top of the tower in medieval times to be replaced as part of the reconstruction programme. It has been erected, as can be seen, although the work was not completed until the 1990s.

A white marble memorial to the Eighth Duke of Argyll and his Duchess lies in the south aisle of the Abbey Church, near the crossing. The Duchess is buried below her effigy, but the coronet at the feet of the Duke indicates that his body was laid to rest elsewhere, in this case in the Argyll family cemetery.

68. The marble memorial to the Eighth Duke of Argyll and the Duchess in the Abbey Church

GEORGE DOVGLAS
VIII DVKE OF ARGYLL
1823 KG·KT 1900

Full credit for the existence of the Iona Community is due to Lord MacLeod. The inspiration, the determination, the persuasiveness and the energy that brought it into being; and the philosophy, mission and ministry of the Community in action: everything sprang from this remarkable churchman.

8. GEORGE MACLEOD & THE IONA COMMUNITY

69. Inset above: Portrait of George MacLeod painted on his retirement from the Iona Community, aged 72, in 1967, by David Donaldson. The painting hangs outside the Abbey library

George MacLeod was born on 17th June, 1895, into a family which had had a distinguished ecclesiastical history for the five previous generations. His grandfather and his great grandfather had been Moderators of the General Assembly of the Church of Scotland, as had other MacLeod forebears close to this direct line. George was brought up in the family home, the manse at Fuinary on the Morven coast four miles west from Lochaline, overlooking the Sound of Mull. He was sent to boarding school first in Edinburgh then at Winchester College. Holidays every August were spent on Iona.

In October, 1913, he went up to Oriel College, Oxford, to read law; but within twelve months Europe was at war and George had taken a commission in the Argyll and Sutherland Highlanders. He spent most of the next four years in the trenches in Flanders, with one short tour in Salonika. He was decorated for bravery by both the British, with an MC, and the French, with the Croix de Guerre.

After the war he decided to abandon his legal studies, having been deeply affected by the widespread slaughter he had witnessed, and work towards ordination. In 1921, aged 26, he took up a post-graduate fellowship at the Union Theology Seminary in New York. On return to Scotland he accepted an Assistantship at St Giles Cathedral in Edinburgh. It was here that his life-long philosophy started to take shape: the acute poverty, and Scotland's worst housing, that he saw around Edinburgh's High Street brought home to him the evils of the 'two nations' of the privileged, and the disadvantaged or deprived. He knew that the Church should provide a sense of community for everyone.

After just three years, in 1924, he was ordained by the Presbytery of Glasgow to be the Toc H full-time padre. Here his resolve to help young people found new scope. He started boys' clubs, and took parties on mountaineering trips. The following year George MacLeod moved again, this time to take up appointment as collegiate minister at Edinburgh's prestigious St Cuthbert's Church. He continued to develop his belief - to persuade all those he saw as his flock 'to apply on weekdays what we sing about on Sundays'.

By this time George MacLeod was a constant whirlwind of energetic activity. He launched many projects not all of which were pleasing to the authorities. He was impatient; outspoken, sometimes outrageously so; wholly dedicated to his campaigns of bringing the Gospel intelligibly to all; and he was a virtuoso preacher, routinely packing his church or hall; and utterly fearless. He was also by now a pacifist. He was accused simultaneously of being Marxist and of being in sympathy with Rome; but he took little notice.

In 1930 he was selected to be the Minister at Govan Old Parish Church beside the decaying shipbuilding area on the south bank of the Clyde three miles downstream from central Glasgow. In Govan he saw afresh all the misery, degradation and despair of poverty, this time brought about by grave, country-wide unemployment. His initiatives here began a sequence that led to the idea of the Iona Community.

But first George MacLeod created a work project for unemployed volunteers to build a garden round the neglected war memorial near the

70. An evening view of the Abbey buildings with the Sound of Iona behind

church, in exchange for a daily hot meal. The sense of community that sprang from this project was impressive. Heartened, he moved up a gear and acquired a ruin called Fingalton Mill out in the country ten miles south-west of Govan. Again unemployed volunteers went to work, this time rebuilding the mill so that it would provide accommodation for 30 temporary residents from the Govan population, bringing them into the fresh air 500 feet up, using an aged bus to take them to and fro. Now to Iona.

George MacLeod knew Iona well, not simply as a place for holidays, but as a historic centre of spirituality, culture and mission. The island surely would be perfect for implementing and extending his vision. In 1935 he made a proposal to the Iona Cathedral Trustees for the reconstruction of the abbey buildings. There was an agonising series of arguments and delays, and George MacLeod had to agree to be personally responsible for all the costs so that the Trustees were at no financial risk, but finally in March, 1938, he was ready to start. The plan was for six new clergy to work as labourers on the site assisting six skilled artisans: in this way the young clergy would be helping to fit themselves for work in deprived urban parishes. Once again war toppled MacLeod's programme. The three month attachments to the Iona project no longer made sense, and for the next six years trainee ministers came for spells of one week. Progress suffered, but was not halted.

The life of the young Community on Iona was not limited to the building tasks, vital though they were: one of the many routines that George MacLeod introduced for the Community was the weekly pilgrimage. On one day every week he would lead a group on a six-mile walk from St Martin's Cross to the Nunnery, on to Loch Staonaig and down to the marble quarry and Saint Columba's Bay, back across the machair and inland to the Hermit's Cell, then to the summit of Dun I and finally back to the Reilig Odhrain. At each of these points he would pause for a prayer. Someone from the Community still leads the pilgrimage every Wednesday morning for all who want to join it.

In the reconstruction of the abbey buildings money was always a problem. Fundraising was necessary for each step, and George MacLeod had to prove solvency before each was authorised. But little by little all the buildings we see today were completed. By 1967 the job was done. Work had received a fillip by the visit of HM The Queen in 1956 when she gave the Abbey Church the oak screen in the north transept; and also when at Whitsun 1963 a huge gathering assembled for the open-air celebration of the fourteenth centenary of Saint Columba's arrival at Iona. In 1968 the Queen Mother came to Iona.

Returning to George MacLeod: the recognition of his achievements spread despite endless squabbles with notables who did not see eye to eye with him. The Iona Community was coming of age, and was starting to be seen as a worldwide vehicle for bringing the Gospel to great numbers of people; and George MacLeod was becoming recognised at home and abroad for his outstanding achievements. In 1956 he was appointed Chaplain to the Queen. In 1957 he became Moderator of the General Assembly of the Church of Scotland. In 1967 the New Year Honours made him a life peer, the first

72. Work in progress on the reconstruction of the abbey buildings in the 1950s

ever Church of Scotland minister to sit in the House of Lords. When George MacLeod retired in September, 1967, from the role he had invented as Leader of the Iona Community, it was as The Very Rev Lord MacLeod of Fuinary DD MC; but he still had 24 years to live, and his restless spirit allowed him to contribute in many ways to the Iona Community and elsewhere until his death at the age of 96 in 1991.

The Rev Norman Shanks, Leader of the Iona Community, has kindly written and contributed the following paragraphs to complete this chapter.

THE IONA COMMUNITY ON THE THRESHOLD OF THE MILLENNIUM

When the rebuilding of Iona Abbey was completed in 1967, many asked what the purpose of the Iona Community was now. But the project that George MacLeod initiated in 1938 to restore the Benedictine monastic ruins was only an outward expression of what the Iona Community was, and still is, all about. One of the Community's favourite prayers expresses the commitment to 'seek new ways to touch the hearts of all', and the Community continues to pursue the same missionary purpose that has inspired it since the outset: it is still about rebuilding, about playing a part in God's work of reshaping the lives of individuals, of the churches, and of wider society.

Iona, of course, remains fundamental to the Community's vocation, our spiritual 'home' with rich memories and associations for all, individually and corporately; and the location too of a very important part of our communal work - two residential centres: Iona Abbey itself, and the MacLeod Centre opened in 1988. In addition to all the other visitors to the island, around one hundred people come from many different backgrounds and countries week by week throughout most of the year to live in these two centres and to explore the significance of the Christian faith in today's world and to share an experience of 'the common life' through working, worshipping and relaxing together.

The members of the Community are not, however, to be discovered on Iona but dispersed throughout Britain and beyond. There has been

73. Walkers on the pilgrimage trail leaving the machair, making their way south to Loch Staonaig

considerable growth and change since the early days. There are now over 220 Members, sharing a common commitment to a five-fold rule, involving a devotional and economic discipline, and a commitment to action for justice and peace. There are almost as many women as men, more lay people than ordained ministers, and, although there are still formal links with the Church of Scotland and the ecumenical bodies, there are many Members from all the other main Christian denominations. The Community is also greatly encouraged by the support of its wider family of over 1500 Associate Members and 1700 Friends.

The Community's administrative headquarters are in Glasgow, still at the Pearce Institute, Govan, which was gifted to the people of Govan as a new community centre by Lady Pearce in 1929 and which has been host to the Iona Community since its first days.

The Community has a staff of almost 50 people, including several Members and Associate Members. The resident group of 25 or so, along with around 30 volunteers from all over the world, run the three centres - the two on Iona, and the Camus adventure camp about three miles away on the Ross of Mull.

More than 20 other staff are based in Glasgow: at the Wild Goose Resource Group, which aims to develop new more participative and accessible approaches to worship, produce liturgical resources, and satisfy the demand for the Group's participation in events throughout Britain and beyond; with Wild Goose Publications, the Community's publishing house; as the youth development worker promoting the Community's concerns among young people; and as administrative and finance support staff.

But the Community has always emphasised the significance of the work that

74. The west face of the abbey church, with St Martin's Cross on the right and St Columba's Shrine and St John's Cross on the left

75. Lord MacLeod, aged 94, at his home in Morven

Members and Associate Members do in their own local situations, through their employment and in their other activities, to live out the concerns and commitment of the Community to finding radical and relevant ways of relating the Christian Gospel to the needs of contemporary society. Current priorities, developing the emphases that have been central to the life of the Community since its outset, relate to the building of the Community, the pursuit of peace-making and social justice, combating poverty and racism, increasing ecumenical understanding, responding to the current widespread interest in spirituality by pointing to the need for an engaged approach that integrates social and spiritual concerns.

So what happens now on Iona is both part of a wider whole and a consistent development of aspects of the original vision and inspiration of George MacLeod. Looking towards the 21st century the Community continues to consider how best to respond to contemporary needs in pursuing its island work. The relationships that have been built over the years both with the local people of Iona, and with the Cathedral trustees who remain responsible for the Abbey Church and the external fabric of the other abbey buildings, provide a good basis for the Community to move forward into the future with creativity and hope.

SPECTACULAR
· ISLAND ·

The appearance of any landscape depends principally on its geology, but the climate will also have had an effect, as will the attentions of man. Geology is apt to be an impenetrable subject to all those who are not specialists, but we need to take a superficial look at the geology of Iona in order to appreciate what we see.

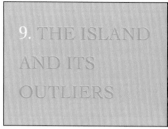

9. THE ISLAND AND ITS OUTLIERS

76. Inset above: Green pebbles, known as St Columba's Tears, which can be found at Columba's Bay

The islands and promontories along the western coast of Scotland were largely fashioned by the intense and prolonged igneous activity occurring roughly 40 million years ago. The Isle of Mull was a centre of major volcanic activity which produced a succession of lava flows, each one typically about 50 feet thick, which solidified to form the basalt plateaus and steps, known as trap country, that give Mull, when seen from any one of several viewpoints, its distinctive terraced silhouettes.

In places where the lava flowed beyond the shores of Mull it has been eroded by the sea, leaving islands of basalt. The Treshnish Isles provide examples, with Fladda and the brim of the Dutchman's Cap exhibiting particularly clear basaltic shelves. Staffa is a sensationally dramatic remnant of the lava flow. Iona, however, is different.

Taking the road westward from Bunessan on Mull the traveller emerges from the dark grey basalt after about a mile, and moves amongst rounded outcrops of pink granite, known as Ross of Mull Granite, until reaching the western extremity of the Ross at Fionnphort. This pink granite ends almost completely at the eastern side

77. The Bull Hole

of the Sound of Iona, but Erraid, the notorious Torran Rocks for long respected by mariners, and all the islets and skerries close to the Ross of Mull are formed of it. One small island in particular, Eilean nam Ban *(pronounced 'El-n-Barn')*, which lies close to the Mull shore of the Sound of Iona consists of this granite: some of the pink stone used in the Abbey and Nunnery was quarried on Eilean

78. Fionnphort on Mull looking towards Dun I on Iona

nam Ban. The name means 'Island of Women' because, it is alleged, at some period women not wanted on Iona were left there. There is a feeble spring-well on the islet so the tale is just plausible. The strip of water lying between Eilean nam Ban and the Ross provides an anchorage called the Bull Hole favoured by yachtsmen; and the Mull-Iona ferry is moored there every night.

The Sound of Iona is about a mile wide with a largely sandy bottom. Over the sand banks, which change their positions slightly from year to year, the water has a depth of only a few feet at low tide. Conditions of wind against tide can cause a steep chop on the surface. On sunny days the shallow sea over the sand is a vivid turquoise: when the Sound is overcast the appearance is likely to be grey and forbidding.

Iona has an area of 1977 acres: the island is 3.4 miles long, 1.6 miles wide at its widest and 0.9 miles wide across its central waist. Aside from the religious buildings, The National Trust for Scotland has title to the whole island including the foreshore.

On crossing the Sound to Iona we find two main types of geological structure. The

80. An Iona beach and the Sound of Iona

western two-thirds of the island consists of extremely old rock called Lewisian Granitic Gneiss, similar to the rock of much of the Outer Hebrides. The geology of the eastern side of Iona is more complicated with a mixture of materials known as conglomerates, grits, and shales. Between these two distinct zones there is a band of rock called Pale Feldspar-rock which carries a seam of marble. The marble, discussed further in Chapter 15, emerges on the shoreline on the eastern edge of the island about a quarter of a mile from its south-east point, and runs inland in an approximately northerly direction. At the seaward end the marble has been quarried from time to time.

79. Boat in an inlet on Eilean nam Ban

Parts of Iona, on both the east and the west, consist of practically level grassland resting on raised beaches. That on the west overlooking the Bay at the Back of the Ocean is the machair, characteristic of many Hebridean islands. As the ice lying on the island shrank back at the close of the last Ice Age 10 to 15 thousand years ago, and the ground no longer had to bear the enormous weight of icefields possibly up to a mile thick, the island rose intermittently some tens of feet, creating the raised beaches. The well drained soil that

81. North end of Iona Sound

formed on these raised beaches made excellent arable land which has been used successfully for crops and grazing since people first settled on the island.

Iona's climate is cool and oceanic. The island has a small temperature range, namely a winter average lying between -2°C and +10°C, and a summer average between 7°C and 20°C, making Iona somewhat milder than Mull, and almost entirely free of snow. Iona also has less rain than most areas of Mull, specifically 55 inches against 80 inches. Strong winds are a feature of Iona, especially on the western side facing the prevailing weather.

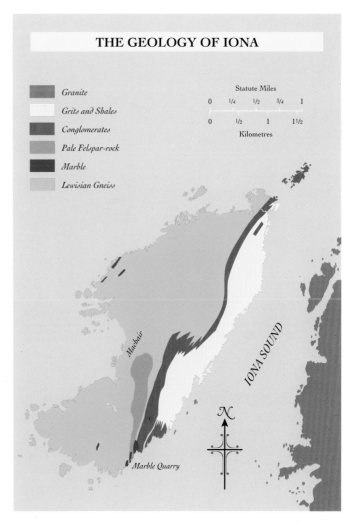

THE GEOLOGY OF IONA

- Granite
- Grits and Shales
- Conglomerates
- Pale Felspar-rock
- Marble
- Lewisian Gneiss

Statute Miles
0   1/4   1/2   3/4   1
0   1/2   1   1 1/2
Kilometres

Machair

IONA SOUND

Marble Quarry

N

There are many islets off Iona, and many more skerries, and other rocks which are covered at high water. The largest islet is Soa two miles to the south-west which until recently has been used for grazing. To the north of Iona, half a mile out, is Storm Island which is linked to a group of off-lying rocks by a conspicuous stable sand spit, about 100 yards in length, which dries at a little above half-tide. This feature is called a tombolo. There are several tombolos around Scotland, one notable one 600 yards long joins St Ninian's Isle to Shetland's Mainland.

The only instances of Ross of Mull granite appearing at Iona are in the chain of islets three-quarters of a mile up the east coast from the marble quarry called Big Island, Rough-skinned Island, and The Red Rock; and in the form of a few erratic boulders on the northern beach called The White Strand of the Monks. Otherwise the break with the pink granite created by the Sound is complete.

The Land

During the time when the Benedictine foundation was flourishing on Iona most of the island's land belonged to the monastery, with the Nunnery owning and making use of the southern end. There then seems to have been a period of some confusion in land use until, in the 18th century, Iona's land was

10. THE LAND & THE SHORE

divided into two areas - the 'East End' consisting of everything north of an east-west line through the Abbey; and 'West End' which was the rest. These terms are in use today, referred to in legal documents as the Townships of East End and West End. The majority of the medieval lay population, however, lived in the area currently occupied by Baile Mor, the formal name of the village.

82. Inset above: Atlantic rollers breaking on the west coast of Iona

The boundary between the townships was established by a stone wall running generally eastwards from behind the parish church; and there are other similar walls here and there on Iona whose purpose is no longer known. One stone dyke that is still plain to see runs from Loch Staonaig in both directions down to the shore.

Apart from the raised beaches and the strip of land running on either side of the road

83. One of the many stone walls which run across the island

84. Sheep grazing on the machair

85. *White sandy beach, east Iona coast, made up of shell fragments which reflect the light*

86. *The White Strand of the Monks, looking towards the village*

across the island to the machair on the west, the island is predominantly hummocky, supporting heather and coarse grasses. The island can thus be considered as having about one third of its surface suitable for cultivation and two thirds as hill-land. Of the former, the most productive sections are the machair and the similar type of area inland from the northern bays. The term machair is used to describe 'soils and vegetation derived from fixed dune pasture and wind-blown sand over native peat', with a high proportion of shell fragments, which is exactly what is found on Iona's raised beaches.

A small amount of the best land is devoted to growing mixed cereal and potatoes, but grass for hay or, increasingly, silage, is much the most popular crop. The hill-land can be used for limited grazing in summer.

There is no significant natural woodland on Iona, mainly because of unregulated grazing long ago and the frequent strong winds, though the large sycamores behind the Heritage Centre seem to do well, and other trees of several kinds survive in the village.

The Shore

The white beaches of Iona, sparkling in the sun, are amongst the most memorable images of the island that the visitor carries away. The beaches themselves, like the raised beaches behind them, consist largely of shell fragments which reflect much of the light striking them.

67

87. The White Strand of the Monks, a pastel drawing by Gordon Menzies

The are no natural harbours or sheltered coves on Iona, so the sandy beaches had an important role for the islanders in days of sail, providing sites where boats could be drawn up clear of the water. There are many small sandy beaches on the east side of the island, below the abbey and the village, which gave the islanders there a choice of safe places to leave their craft.

Starting from the north end of the island and tracking clockwise we can take in the main beaches. The first we reach is the large White Strand of the Monks mentioned in Chapter 3. There are several little stretches of sand to be seen as we work our way south, with Saint Ronan's Bay the next beach of good size lying just north of the current jetty. Beyond the jetty is Martyrs' Bay, also mentioned in Chapter 3, followed by a string of beaches, including an attractive one called Sandeels Bay, reaching half way from the village to the marble quarry.

Quarter of a mile round the south-east point of the island is Columba's Bay. This bay is not sandy but shingly. It is split by a rock

88. Port Ban

89. A view from the Bay at the Back of the Ocean showing the Treshnish Isles on the horizon

outcrop into two parts of which the more southerly, known as The Port of the Coracle, is supposed to be the spot where Saint Columba first landed on Iona in the year 563. Pursuing our route round the south-west promontory of the island, after almost a mile we come to the large sandy beach on the Bay at the Back of the Ocean beside the machair.

A short way beyond the northern end of the machair is Port Ban, a beautiful inlet with a gently shelving foreshore, tucked in below Dun Bhuirg. Finally, there is a splendid beach at Calva, half a mile in extent, running eastwards back to our starting point. Approximately, half of Iona's coastline is sandy.

90. Looking from Iona towards the Gribun cliffs on Mull

The drop in the level of the sea relative to the land which brought about the raised beaches has been reversed, probably by two effects of gradually rising temperatures - the inflow of melted polar ice, and the increased volume occupied by warmer seawater. The sea level is at present rising at a rate of about two inches each decade. The encroaching sea threatens the dunes which support the raised beaches. To protect the most vulnerable lengths of beach

91. Calva Beach

the National Trust for Scotland has deployed volunteers working from the Trust's Thistle Camps to plant marram grass to help stabilise the dunes.

Between the beaches the shoreline is rocky, and often steep and slippery. There are several caves and other features of interest along these stretches of coast. Two are of particular interest: the marble quarry which is described in Chapter 15, and which can be reached by following a gully down from a point midway between Loch Staonaig and Columba's Bay; and the Spouting Cave, a fissure in the rock at the southern extremity of the Bay at the Back of the Ocean which creates a vertical jet of water when it is struck by a wave of suitable size. The Spouting Cave performs most dramatically at about half-tide when there is a shapely sea fetching from the west.

92. Looking northward from Calva beach towards Mull and Ulva

93. The Spouting Cave

The flora of Iona is similar to that of other Hebridean islands, but more varied than that on most. It resembles closely the flora of the outer islands which are largely formed of old gneiss rock of the kind that underlies the majority of Iona. The climate of Iona also resembles that of most of the more westerly islands, being windy, mild, dark in winter and light in summer, and not nearly as wet as, for instance, Mull or Skye.

Here we present a portrait of some of the flowers that can usually be seen on Iona in spring or early summer. This selection has been made not against any botanical or other scientific criteria but on the basis of their pictorial variety; and it is restricted to species that can be observed most years. The 1993 edition of Jean Millar's Book *Flowers of Iona* lists more than 400 species, including rushes, sedges, grasses, and ferns. A few of them are peculiar to Iona, and nearly all of them occur naturally in the wild, though the total range is augmented by some which have escaped from domestic gardens.

11. FLOWERS

94. Inset above: **Bog Pimpernel** *(Anagallis tenella)*

95. Watercolour by Jan Fisher of Thrift, or Sea Pinks, on the beach at the north-east tip of Iona looking over Storm Island towards high ground on Mull

97. **Yarrow or Milfoil** *(Achillea millefolium)*

As well as being a flower Yarrow is a herb with a long tradition of providing cures for a wide range of injuries and illnesses. It is found in meadows, on banks, and beside roads.

100. **Marsh Cinquefoil**
(Potentilla palustris)

96. **English Stonecrop**
(Sedum anglicum)

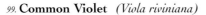

98. **Marsh Marigold or Kingcup** *(Caltha palustris)*

The Marsh Marigold appears in spring with bright golden flowers, and is usually found beside streams and in damp hollows in fields and ditches.

99. **Common Violet** *(Viola riviniana)*

This dainty plant with purple flowers can occur in a range of sizes. It is seen on hillsides. When there were wooded slopes on Iona the Common Violet would perhaps have been be more abundant.

101. **Early Purple Orchid**
(Orchis mascula)

105. Wood Anemone *(Anemone nemorosa)*

The Wood Anemone is one of the earliest spring plants to flower. It thrives in moist areas, and is a robust species because its rootstock continuously extends itself and is able to provide new sources of shoots. It contains a poisonous substance with the name of protoanemonine.

102. **Sneezewort**

(Achillea ptarmica)

105. **Marsh Thistle**

(Cirsium palustre)

104. Heather or Ling *(Calluna vulgaris)*

Ling decorates hillsides with its tiny purple, or occasionally white, flowers from July until October. It flourishes in damp, cool conditions, and is tolerant of the salt air of maritime climates. It grows strongly on Iona.

106. **Bulbous Buttercup**
(Ranunculus bulbosus)

107. **Scottish Bluebell** *(Campanula rotundifolia)*

The Scottish Bluebell or Harebell grows most often on dry grassland, on rocks, and at the edges of tracks; and occasionally on walls. There are several varieties of the Harebell: it sometimes carries white flowers in place of the normal violet or blue ones.

109. **Red Campion**
(Silene dioica)

108. **Cuckoo Flower or Lady's Smock** *(Cardamine pratensis)*

In dry conditions the lilac-coloured flowers can be seen in damp areas and along the banks of streams. In rain, and at night, the flowers fold themselves away. White froth can often be observed on the stems of Cuckoo Flower. This is called cuckoo spit.

110. **Bog Asphodel**
(Narthecium ossifragum)

111. **Long-headed Poppy**
(Papaver dubium)

115. **Red Clover** *(Trifolium pratense)*

113. **Birdsfoot-trefoil or Bacon and Eggs**
(Lotus corniculatus)

The Birdsfoot-trefoil grows abundantly in fields and on open pasture, particularly the Iona machair. It is regarded as being good feed for animals, both while growing and after cutting.

112. **Ragged Robin** *(Lychnis flos-cuculi)*

Although the Ragged Robin is not prolific on Iona, its strongly-coloured pink-red flowers can sometimes be seen in good numbers on marshy ground and in damp corners of fields.

116. **Spear Thistle**
(Cirsium vulgare)

114. **Wood-sorrel or Sheep's Sorrel** *(Oxalis acetosella)*

Wood-sorrel favours land with decaying vegetable matter, and does well on hill ground. It is said to be poisonous to sheep in spring. At night its leaves and flowers close by folding inward.

117. **Yellow Flag or Iris**
(Iris pseudacorus)

118. **Thrift or Sea Pink**
(Armeria maritima)

120. **Primrose** *(Primula vulgaris)*

119. **Bloody Cranesbill**
(Geranium sanguineum)

121. **Lesser Celandine or Pilewort** *(Ranunculus ficaria)*

The Lesser Celandine flourishes, forming dense clumps, in ground with ample humus whether on high ground or on low-lying sites with plentiful moisture such as stream banks. The leaves of young plants are sometimes used for salads because of the Vitamin C they contain.

122. **Bell Heather** *(Erica cinerea)*

123. **Foxglove** *(Digitalis purpurea)*

126. *Risso's Dolphin*

Throughout the final quarter of the 20th century the bookshop in Tobermory, on the Isle of Mull, has maintained records of sightings of marine mammals. Realising that positive identification is not always possible, and that populations of these mammals may vary in size and in the pattern of movement they adopt from year to year, the following selection is far from a guarantee that anyone can see all of them on any one excursion, or even all in one season, on the waters around Mull and Iona. Nor are the entries below intended provide the information needed for certain recognition: rather they try to show the richness of the diversity to be found around these shores.

12. MARINE LIFE

124. *Inset above: Common Seals*

Mentioned below are whales, dolphins, and porpoises called collectively *cetaceans;* seals which belong to the family *phocoidea;* and the basking shark which, incidentally, is a fish, not a mammal, included because it is a fine sea creature, seen frequently; and the rare otter.

127. *Orca, or Killer Whale*

Whales

The Orca, or **Killer Whale** *(Orcinus orca),* is a strikingly marked mammal: the black parts are jet black, and the white parts brilliant white. It is up to about 30 feet long, thick and yet streamlined. Technically the Orca is classified as a dolphin as its mouth is equipped with snugly-fitting conical teeth. Nonetheless it is harmless to human beings: its label of Killer is a tribute to its efficiency as a predator. The Orca is gregarious, often moving in a pod of ten or more, and seems at home in every ocean of the world.

125. *Minke Whale*

The **Minke Whale** (*Balaenoptera acutorostrata*), grows to almost the same length as the Orca but is much sleeker. Regarded as insignificant by whale-catchers until recently, the Minke is now prized, especially by the Japanese, for its meat.

The **Long-finned Pilot Whale** (*Globicephala melaena*), in contrast to the two whale species described above, has a blunt stubby head reminiscent of the symbols used on displays for depicting whales of unspecified type. All pilot whales form large groups, but the Long-finned species congregate into herds that range from a few hundreds to several thousands. Each whale is capable of a speed of 25 miles an hour.

Dolphins

In their booklet '*Was it a Whale?*' the authors Jay Butler and Anna Levin provide illustrations and descriptions of six species of dolphin, all to be seen on occasion in Hebridean waters: the **Common Dolphin** (*Delphinus delphis*), the **Bottlenose Dolphin** (*Tursiops truncatus*), **Risso's Dolphin** (*Grampus griseus*), the **White-beaked Dolphin** (*Lagenorhynchus albirosis*), the **Atlantic White-sided Dolphin** (*Lagenorhynchus acutus*), and the **Striped Dolphin** (*Stenella coeruleoalba*). Most of these move in groups, so whenever you spot a dolphin there is a likelihood that you will soon enjoy a display by a number, perhaps a large number, of them.

128. *Bottlenose Dolphin*

The **Harbour**, or **Common Porpoise** (*Phocoena phocoena*) is smaller than the dolphins, growing to no more than six feet in length. It does not have a beak, a feature which characterises nearly all dolphins. Unlike the dolphins it usually travels singly or in pairs, and rarely leaps out of the water.

Porpoises

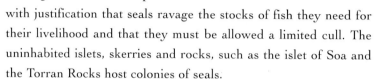

Seals

Ahigh proportion of the boat trips which set out to find seals around Iona are successful. The seal population is probably growing thanks to restrictions on commercial exploitation, although fishermen complain with justification that seals ravage the stocks of fish they need for their livelihood and that they must be allowed a limited cull. The uninhabited islets, skerries and rocks, such as the islet of Soa and the Torran Rocks host colonies of seals.

The sight of seals sunning themselves is treasured by holidaymakers who empathise with the round, baby-like features, the labrador-style eyes, and the friendly demeanour.

Worldwide there are 32 species of seal. Of those, only two are found in the Hebrides; and both are well represented. In appearance these species are similar to one another, both having mottled backs and appearing black, grey or brown.

The **Common**, or **Harbour Seal** *(Phoca vitulina)*, grows to about five feet in length with a weight of a little over 200 pounds.

The **Grey**, or **Atlantic Seal** *(Halichoerus grypus)*, is less tubby than the Common Seal, and is rather longer, growing to eight feet. Its head is also longer giving the Grey Seal a kind of aristocratic nose.

129. Top: Common Seal
130. Above: Grey Seal

131. Basking Shark

Basking Shark *(Cetorhinus maximus).* Despite its forbidding name the basking shark is harmless. It is, however, large. It can reach 30 feet in length, and can weigh four tons. Fishermen sometimes call it the 'sunfish' because of its habit of lying with its back above the water apparently enjoying the sunshine. To feed, the Basking Shark will cruise slowly with its mouth fully open, scooping up huge volumes of plankton-laden water.

Sharks

Otter *(Lutra lutra).* Although the Otter is exceptionally shy, one is occasionally seen in the sea or ashore.

Otters

81

Professor Estlin Waters, an authority on the birds of the Hebrides, has kindly written and contributed this chapter.

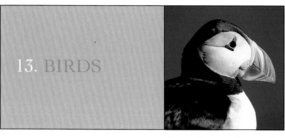

13. BIRDS

132. Inset above: Puffin

From Iona the visitor can readily go out to Staffa, or to the Treshnish Isles or, indeed, to both on the same excursion, whenever the sea is calm and the weather settled. Boat trips serve both these areas, allowing passengers to observe a variety of birds, often in substantial colonies. The Gannet, Britain's largest seabird, may be seen. Their nearest breeding colony is on Ailsa Craig, but gannets forage widely and their plunge-dives after fish are spectacular. It may be possible to see some distant migrants, especially in spring and autumn; an unusual Shearwater or Skua is always a possibility.

On most sailing days in summer landing is possible on Staffa, and also on Lunga in the Treshnish Isles. There may be reward for circumnavigating islands, rather than landing on them, to gain excellent views of large colonies of nesting seabirds. However, climbing ashore allows a sight of the land birds that inhabit these windswept islands.

Iona

The visitor to Iona might expect the birds of Iona to have become well known and thoroughly documented, because of the relative ease of access. Indeed, that was the case when, in 1848, an Englishman, Henry Davenport Graham, came to live for several years on the island. After his death his careful observations of Iona and its surrounding sea areas, together with his characteristic

133. Shags on a rock close to Eilean nam Ban in autumn

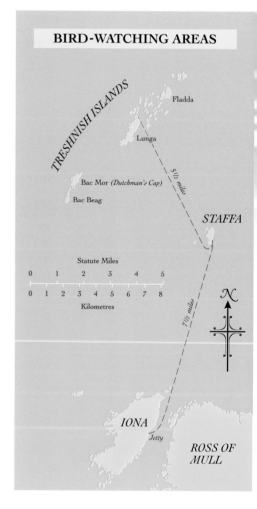

BIRD-WATCHING AREAS

TRESHNISH ISLANDS

Fladda

Lunga

Bac Mor *(Dutchman's Cap)*

Bac Beag

STAFFA

5½ miles

7½ miles

Statute Miles

0   1   2   3   4   5

0   1   2   3   4   5   6   7   8

Kilometres

N

IONA

Jetty

ROSS OF MULL

134. Gannet

drawings, were published in a book of nearly 300 pages titled *'The Birds of Iona & Mull'*.

Although this is a long time ago, the present standard book *'Birds in Scotland'*, by Valerie Thom, cites Graham's book as giving the most up-to-date check list for Iona. Graham provides a good base to which scattered reports, including some in *'Scottish Bird Report'* and *'Argyll Bird Report'*, can be added; but a detailed, comprehensive list is wanted. In particular, records in the winter months are needed.

Iona has fewer seabirds than, say, the Treshnish Isles, but Fulmar, Shag and Kittiwake breed on the south-western cliffs - a part of the island barely within range of the day tourist.

The land bird of most interest on Iona is the Corn

135. Kittiwake

Crake. This summer visitor has greatly decreased in numbers and in breeding range in Britain. It is found in hay meadows and rough pastures where it usually keeps itself well concealed. It is rarely seen to fly, which makes the long winter migration to sub-Saharan Africa rather surprising.

The skulking Corn Crake is detected by the distinctive double rasping note of the male 'arp...arp', sometimes repeated endlessly. He calls most on summer evenings, often continuing through the night. While no birdwatcher is likely to describe it so today, Graham says that it can be 'wearisome', and that he was sometimes urged to turn out at night with his gun to 'dislodge this murderer of my sleep'. He adds that 'they are very good eating; indeed, the game-laws include them under the head of game'. A survey in 1978 found about 25 calling Corn Crakes on

158. Buzzard

Iona. This number declined greatly, but a few pairs return each May to breed: in 1997 there were eight calling Corn Crakes, an increase over counts a few years earlier.

137. Habitat for the Corn Crake

Another bird that has a contracting range is the Twite. It occurs particularly on islands and joins together in flocks from August onwards. Flocks of several hundred birds have been recorded on Iona, mainly in September. The Twite is said to be resident all year on Iona but it may be scarce in winter. I saw none during two sunny days walking the island in November, 1998.

Other common birds on Iona include Buzzard, Rock Dove, Starling, Hooded Crow and Jackdaw. In the 19th century Jackdaws bred on the tower of the Abbey Church. Rooks were first recorded breeding in the trees around the manse in 1944, and this rookery thrives today with 30 or 40 nests. The Chough, formerly known as the red-legged crow, is now uncommon in Scotland. In the middle of the 19th century Graham recorded three pairs as constantly resident, 'one pair being permitted to breed in St Columba's tower by the colony of Jackdaws while the other two bred in a sea cave', their more usual site.

Choughs have been seen in recent years on Mull, although breeding there has not been successful.

139. Hooded Crow

140. Sanderling

Visitors should keep their eyes and ears open: the Chough's note resembles that of the Jackdaw but is longer, more musical and higher pitched. Long gone are the days when choughs were shot. Graham shot several and each time he 'was obliged to shoot at its mate also, partly out of pity for her grief and also because I felt rather ashamed of myself...'.

As well as numerous resident Oystercatchers, waders are frequent during migration and many species have been seen. In Argyll generally, the Sanderling is an uncommon passage migrant although there are several records from the sandy beaches of Iona. Just offshore Eider and Red-breasted Merganser often swim close to low rocks.

One of the interests of visiting small islands is to see what are often regarded as garden or woodland birds such as Blackbirds, Song Thrushes, Robins, Wrens and Hedge Accentors (dunnocks or hedge sparrows). On Iona these species live in an often bare and windswept environment, not regarded by most birdwatchers as their usual habitat, although they also use remote crofts and gardens in the village. The Hedge Accentor of the Hebrides has been

142. Eider Duck

141. Oystercatcher

143. Opposite page:
Red-breasted Merganser

144. Razorbill

described as a separate subspecies (*Prunella modularis hebridium*) as it has darker markings above and darker grey underparts which extend further down the belly. This subspecies breeds in heather and bracken, often well away from gardens, but occasionally in gardens.

Wrens inhabit gardens and stone walls on Iona, but also occur well away from them. Even in winter, Wrens move along wet ditches beside the island's roads with only short reedy vegetation for cover. As elsewhere Wrens are probably much reduced in numbers by hard winters.

Staffa

Staffa is an island of about 70 acres, best known for its world-famous Fingal's Cave. It has several colonies of seabirds: Shags, Fulmars, Puffins and Razorbills are all likely to be seen. There is a stairway leading from the landing place to the island's plateau which offers an excellent view of the surrounding seascape as well as the habitat for several species of birds. Those climbing up may see Starlings and Wheatears and, around the edge of the plateau,

145. Fulmar

146. Fulmar chick

147. *Cormorant drying its wings*

Rock Pipits. This is a good site for the Purple Sandpiper, especially in May when they might be on the rocks where the waves are breaking. Storm-petrels breed on Staffa, but they are unlikely to be seen by the day visitor.

Treshnish Isles

The Treshnish Isles are widely known for their outstanding seabird colonies. This archipelago of about 20 small islands and a very large number of rocks lies as a chain six miles long running south-westward from Treshnish Point on Mull. Their total area is about 300 acres. Lunga is the largest island of the chain, offering the best landfall and also the finest opportunities for observing seabirds. It consists of about 200 acres of shapely land rising to 338 feet. As well as being home to its many colonies of seabirds it supports several of the flowers illustrated in Chapter 11, and it is a noted breeding ground for Grey Seals.

It was on Lunga that Fraser Darling camped and first studied the Grey Seal, writing about his experiences in his popular 1940 book *'Island Years'*.

Many hundreds of pairs of Fulmars breed on the Treshnish Isles, their numbers fluctuating considerably from year to year. Most nest on Lunga, with the Dutchman's Cap three miles down the chain to the south-west, also popular with Fulmars.

Shags nest on several of the islands, with the largest number on Lunga where there are usually well over 100 pairs. Cormorants are much less common, and do not breed on the Treshnish Isles. Of the auks the Guillemot is the most numerous with several thousand pairs, most of which breed on Harp Rock just off Lunga. The Razorbill is more scattered on the

148. *Shag*

Treshnish Isles, but with a total of many hundreds of breeding pairs. The Black Guillemot (or tystie) is much less numerous and is most likely to be seen swimming on the sea: sometimes more than 30 pairs breed, although only a single bird was seen in 1997.

Of all the seabirds the Puffin is many people's favourite. It breeds on several of the islands with the largest number on Lunga where it has been increasing over recent years with now more than 1,800 pairs. The

149. Black Guillemot

Kittiwake is the true sea gull, and comes ashore mainly to breed. It too seems to be increasing in numbers. Its chief breeding colony is on Lunga's Harp Rock where, in 1997, there were 735 pairs.

Of the other gulls, the Herring Gull is the most numerous with a few hundred pairs spread over several islands. The Great Black-backed Gull is easily the next commonest with perhaps 100 pairs. There are smaller numbers of Lesser Black-backed Gulls and Common Gulls. The distinction between the Arctic Tern and the Common Tern foxes many

150. Great Black-backed Gull

151. Puffins

birdwatchers. One difference is on the bill: the Arctic Tern has no dark tip to its red bill. Both species occur frequently, and other species of tern have been seen in the area. There is an irregular colony of terns with both Arctic and Common species breeding, but they appear not to breed every year. In 1996 there was a mixed colony of several hundred of these two species of terns at Sgeirean na Guisaich, a group of rocks a little north-east of Lunga.

Two other seabirds are common nesters on the Treshnish Isles yet are unlikely to be seen by day visitors because they come ashore to their underground nests after dark. They are Manx Shearwaters and Storm-petrels. No accurate estimate of the numbers of Manx Shearwaters seems to have been made but possibly several hundred pairs nest in burrows on the slopes of the north-east side of Lunga, and breeding may also occur on the Dutchman's Cap. Sometimes, especially on calm evenings, Manx Shearwaters may be seen gathering offshore, maybe resting on the sea, waiting for the cover of darkness to fly ashore. Fraser Darling describes the nocturnal cries of the Manx Shearwater as a cracked, half-choked scream; and a night among them is one to be remembered.

152. Common Tern

153. Manx Shearwater

154. Corn Crake

Much smaller, but more numerous than the Manx Shearwater, is the Storm-petrel. This bird arrives and leaves its colonies at night. It is even less likely to be seen by visitors during the day though those with sharp eyes may catch sight of it occasionally as it dances low over the waves, usually well away from land. It breeds in boulder beaches, burrows, stone walls and deserted buildings. It is from this cover that the petrels call persistently at night - an uneven purring, sometimes likened to a distant Nightjar, followed by a series of abrupt 'chikka' sounds, once described as sounding like a fairy being sick.

Using a tape recording of this call, and noting the Storm-petrel's ready reply to the recording, an accurate estimate of the Treshnish population was made between 9th and 29th July, 1996. The results were published in '*Scottish Birds*' (1998, 19, 145-153). The estimate was 5,040 pairs widely spread over the islands at 57 sites, but with more than half on the island of Fladda two miles north-east of Lunga.

Arctic Skuas are sometimes seen on Harp Rock, and a pair of Great Skuas (bonxies) were suspected of nesting on Fladda in 1996.

Greylag Geese occur in small flocks every summer and Barnacle Geese in large flocks in winter. The only regular breeding duck is the Eider, with small numbers nesting on several of the islands.

Other birds regularly seen in summer include Buzzard, Corn Crake, Oystercatcher, Ringed Plover, Common Sandpiper, Snipe, Rock Dove, and several species of small land birds such as Pied Wagtail, Wheatear, Starling and Twite. Three pairs of Twite normally breed on Lunga, with others on Fladda and Dutchman's Cap. There can be surprises: a Golden Eagle appeared on Fladda in 1993, and an Alpine Swift on Lunga in 1994.

155. Storm-petrel

The size of Iona's population has undergone notable fluctuations over the past 250 years. Estimates before about the year 1800 are rough, partly because those making them tended to count the number of families, and then multiply that figure by the supposed total of adults and children in a typical family.

14. THE POPULATION OF IONA

156. Inset above: The landward end of the jetty in about 1890

We can, though, see a growth in numbers from between 250 and 300 in the second half of the 18th century to around 500 in the 1830s. Thereafter there was decline, abrupt at first mainly on account of the potato crisis, to under 250 by 1870. Until the 1920s the population then stayed between 200 and 250.

There was another pronounced drop in the 1920s, bringing the average for the following 75 years down to 135. The latest population figure available is just below 100. This most recent decline is not necessarily a pointer to further falls. There are in fact pointers towards the opposite outcome: for example, the Island of Foula, far out in the Atlantic to the west of Shetland and much more lonely than Iona, arrested its fall in population when it reached 32 a few years ago, and has apparently devised a sustainable life-style for the islanders whose population has now

157. The Iona village street, with the sand of St. Ronan's Bay to the left and the Abbey Church to the right

risen to 42; closer to Iona, the Isle of Ulva was down to three residents in the 1960s but now has more than 25. In the Northern Isles there are several cases, including Fair Isle, Papa Stour, Fetlar, and Out Skerries where populations of less than 100 appear perfectly stable.

158. Activity on the jetty, about 1900

Modern electronic communication systems, and modern air and sea links, seem to offer viability to these communities that hitherto felt themselves to be uncomfortably isolated.

The ownership of Iona has, of course, always been a matter of concern to the residents. In March, 1979, the Trustees of the 10th Duke of Argyll announced that they intended to dispose of the Duke's interests in the island. The whole island apart from the religious sites was acquired by the Hugh Fraser Foundation for the nation in May of that year, and in November, 1979, The National Trust for Scotland was invited, with the approval of the Hugh Fraser Foundation, to accept ownership. There were many questions of feus, leases, and tenancies to be settled, but on

159. The village street in about 1910

1st March, 1980, the transfer of title took place at a price of £1,100,245, supported by an endowment.

The best guide to the structure of the population following the change in ownership is provided by the 1991 census. At the time of the count there were 80 dwellings on the island of which 41 housed the 130 residents. Of the 39 other properties 20 were 'holiday accommodation', six were empty, two were second homes, two belonged to the National Trust for Scotland, and there were nine 'other'.

The declarations for adults showed that 50 were employed full-time, six part-time, 25 were self-employed, and 27 had retired, making 108, which allows for a figure of 22 minors and others not included for a variety of reasons. None were unemployed. In the next chapter we look at some of the activities that the islanders have embraced over the years.

161. Opposite page: Dawn behind the war memorial at the northern end of Martyrs' Bay

160. The village street in 1998

We start this chapter on a sombre note.

In the early morning of 13th December, 1998, there was a terrible and deeply tragic accident in the Sound of Iona in which four of the island's young men were drowned. The impact of the loss of these four lives on the tiny population of Iona, where each person knows all the others, will necessarily be painful and long-lasting. Iona may never fully recover from this disaster. No thought can be given to the activities of the people of Iona without pausing to pay respect to the memory of these men. Two of them were involved in the small-scale commercial fishing operations carried out from Iona, so it is appropriate to begin by looking at the role of fishing, and its importance for the islanders.

15. ISLAND ACTIVITIES

Fishing

Years ago, the sea used to provide food for everyone on the island, and every family was practised at fishing. This impressive list of fish in Iona waters in the 19th century was furnished painstakingly by a visitor: 'turbot, halibut, skate, sole, plaice, flounders, salmon, cod, ling, gurnet, sea trout, mackerel, and herrings, in the sea, and on the bottom lobsters, crabs, and lesser-known kinds of shell-fish'. In times of shortage the presence of copious stocks of fish provided a valuable buffer against starvation; and at other times surpluses could be exported from the island.

Latterly, stocks have dwindled. Since the lengthy list above was drawn up not only have the quantities available shrunk, but regulations that discourage most kinds of fishing have been introduced.

What the future will bring we must wait to learn.

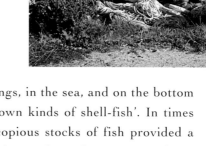

163. Lobster creels and buoys beside the jetty

162. Inset above: Cultivating plants for the island and for sale

*164. Light craft drawn up ashore
at St. Ronan's Bay*

The Kirk

From the mid-16th century when the monks and nuns left Iona, and the Abbey Church and the Nunnery started to suffer from neglect, the inhabitants had no place for collective worship until 1830. That year the Iona Church of Scotland parish church designed by Thomas Telford was completed and brought into use. In the meanwhile some of the people used the abandoned Abbey Church for private prayer.

Telford had a commission from the government to build 32 churches and 43 manses in remote parishes in the Highlands and Islands, within a total budget of £54,000, allied to a scheme of road and bridge construction intended to improve communications and thus encourage people to stay in these areas.

The Iona parish church and manse together cost £1,503. The church is normally open; the manse is currently leased to the Iona Heritage Trust, and is the home of the Heritage Centre. On the Isle of Ulva 12

*165. Inside the parish church
looking east*

166. The Iona parish church built by Thomas Telford in 1828/9

miles to the north there is another of the Telford churches; others are on Mull, Islay, Skye, Harris, North Uist, and at Quarff on Shetland and at North Ronaldsay on Orkney. Bearing in mind the difficulties of transporting building materials and, indeed, of movement generally, at that time, the construction of these churches and manses represents an astonishing achievement.

With the 'Disruption' of 1843 the Church of Scotland Free, as it called itself, broke away entirely from the Presbyterian Church. Across Scotland one third of the people and 40% of the ministers of the old Kirk joined the new. At first the congregation of the Free Church on Iona had no regular place of worship but after a few years they were able to build and use a chapel, now a private house, standing at the southern end of Martyrs' Bay. In 1929 the two followings came together again, and the combined congregation has since then held its divine services in the parish church, at present every Sunday.

A little north of the village street lies the Bishop's House, which was founded as an Episcopalian retreat-house in 1894. It contains its own Chapel of Saint Columba which lies behind the rose window, accommodation, and meeting rooms.

There is a Roman Catholic place for worship and meetings in a house towards the south-west edge of the village.

167. The Bishop's House at the northern edge of the village

Dr Johnson noted at the time of his visit to Iona in 1773 that there was no school. However the following year a schoolmaster was recruited and, it is said, that by the end of his first year he had 40 pupils. A visitor to Iona in 1788 reported that there were then 25 pupils from an island population of about 300; twenty years later there were 30 in school, in 1877 there were 57, and in 1896, 41.

Schooling

Following the rout of the Jacobites at Culloden in April, 1746, the Act of Prescription which amongst many stern measures banned the teaching of Gaelic, was speedily drafted, and brought into force in 1747. It was repealed 35 years later in 1782, but by that time a whole generation had been deprived of the possibility of learning the Gaelic, which had previously been the universal language on Iona. This may partly explain why Johnson found no education in progress on the island.

*169. An Iona farmhouse,
byre and steading*

In painful contrast to the organised schooling which seems to have burgeoned in the mid-1770s, and lasted for two hundred years, by the end of the 20th century there were no children of primary school age living on the island. Older children attend secondary school in Oban, coming home at weekends. The Iona school building is being preserved against the day when a fresh cohort of five-year-olds can be received into the classroom.

*168. Sheep on the beach beside
the machair*

Iona is a fertile island. Visitors in the 18th and 19th centuries reported seeing barley, oats, flax and rye, standing though not necessarily all at the same time; and potatoes, turnips and other vegetables growing, with surplus that was exported. Kelp and other seaweed, or tangle, was gathered from the shore both to fertilise fields and for sale after being reduced to ash. Horses, cattle, sheep, and pigs were in evidence.

Agriculture

A visitor in 1857 reported the pasture on Iona to be excellent as testified by the quality of the milk and butter. He also said that

*170. Grazing found at the edge of the
road which runs across the island*

101

there were too many individual holdings to allow efficient use of the land, and a marked reluctance to modernise equipment or techniques of farming. Apparently at that time there were no boundaries between the croft areas, allowing animals to wander, leading to frequent disputes.

The pattern of land use has altered gradually but continuously over the years, and most conspicuously since 1945. Nearly all the arable land has been put to grass, destined to be silage or hay in quantities determined by the weather. Some families grow potatoes, but there is certainly no excess for general sale. The number of cattle, and the proportion of cattle to sheep, have both dwindled and continue to do so. At the beginning of the 20th century most crofting families kept a breeding sow: now none do.

171. Harvesting oats on Iona

172. *A watercolour by Julia Wroughton of corn stooks on Iona*

Sheep do well on Iona. On the lower ground the Blue Leicester-Blackface cross, mated with Suffolk tups, produce large strong animals; and on the rough pasture higher up, the Blackface are successful.

There are two farms and 18 crofts on the Island, with the National Trust for Scotland the superior landlord. The effect of this arrangement is that the Trust has some inalienable rights, but day-to-day agriculture works in a benign and productive fashion. The distinction between a farm and a croft is a technical one based on the nature of the leasehold and tenancy agreements made with the National Trust for Scotland.

173. *Corn drying, with Mull on the horizon*

Tourism

There was little demand for a ferry service across the Sound of Iona before the age of the car and the motor coach. A timetabled ferry began operating around 1850, but until the end of the century it consisted of a small single-sail craft. There had been paddle-steamer sailings to Iona from further afield since 1830. As the demand to see the island, stimulated by Queen Victoria's visit in 1847, grew, most tourists were brought by steamer from either Oban or Glasgow. At Iona they were put ashore by lighter. One such cruise from Oban, furnished by the turbine steamer King George V, operated until 1976.

In 1850 the first jetty was built on Iona. It was one of the results of a programme of publicly-funded works on the island designed to provide a measure of financial relief in the wake of the potato blight. Since then there have been successive improvements to the jetty, converting it latterly into a concrete slipway for the modern ferry. The capacity and style of working of the ferry service have marched forward to meet the swelling demand by passengers to cross Iona Sound. The numbers coming to Iona, though constrained by the two wars, otherwise showed continuous growth throughout the 20th century.

174. Bookshop, Iona

175. A yacht at anchor off
St. Ronan's Bay

*177. The turbine steamer
King George V
in Iona Sound*

178. Alongside the old pier on Mull

*176. The Iona ferry under sail,
about 1900*

The great majority of those who cross to Iona are day visitors, but the ferry is also used by holiday-makers staying for longer than a few hours, by people who work on Iona but live on Mull, delivery drivers, emergency and administrative staff, commuting schoolchildren, and no doubt other categories of passengers. Records are kept of the total numbers crossing on the ferry, week by week and year by year. The annual figure doubled between the mid-1980s and the late-1990s to almost 300,000.

On a typical day in August 2,500 passengers, nearly all tourists, cross each way on the ferry; and in addition some will reach the island from chartered yachts and other independent craft. Iona responds by offering them the sacred buildings that most have come to see, refreshment, information, space and quiet, and the intangible, undefinable attraction of this special place. Somehow the island manages to absorb these throngs in a way that lets everyone go away fulfilled.

Shooting

For a glimpse of the pursuit of game on Iona we can read from the entries of a diarist writing in the middle of the 19th century. He must have been spoiled for choice elsewhere, for he claims that on Iona game was not plentiful - just a few woodcocks, snipe, wild duck, and some rabbits; also, a golden eagle occasionally, and Norwegian rats which seemed to be at home on the island. Hawks were said to abound.

Some years later H.D.Graham's book *'The Birds of Iona & Mull'* mentioned in Chapter 13, which is dedicated to 'The Birds of Iona:

all shot upon that Sacred Island or in its vicinity', published in Edinburgh in 1890 and now a minor classic, has drawings of himself shooting many kinds of birds including one with the caption 'Shooting Kestrels in the Cathedral'.

Golf

An 18-hole golf course of 4,600 yards has been laid out on the machair. The course is flat, and apt to be windy; but its setting around the Bay at the Back of the Ocean is stunning. There are no man-made hazards, because there are enough natural ones to satisfy all but the most masochistic, and there is no club house. Every August there is a competition played over 11 holes, with each player scoring the best nine so that there is allowance for problems caused by, for example, freely-roaming animals.

180. Golf on the machair: putting out on the third

Quarrying the Marble

In Chapter 9 we noted the seam of marble running out to the coast near the extreme south-east of the island. The marble itself is appealing: it is a white stone with a clear green vein providing irregular patterns on all faces. Exploitation of this attractive and readily saleable marble has had an uneasy history.

The altar, or Communion Table, in the medieval Abbey Church had been finely sculptured from Iona marble, but soon after the Reformation it was broken up and the many pieces became scattered. However the quarry must have been worked before then to have provided the stone in the first place. It is known that the quarry was active for a short time towards the end of the 18th century, and again definitely between 1907 and 1914. The most severe difficulty faced by all the various operators of the quarry was that of conveying the blocks and slabs of marble from the quarry to the market. Everything had to go by sea from the quarry site, and as no quay of any kind existed

179. The communion table in the Abbey Church

181. Opposite page: Blocks of quarried marble still awaiting shipment. The seated figure gives scale

182. The Fielding and Platt gas engine installed at the quarry in 1911

183. The foundations of quarrymen's dwellings close to the quarry

movement was constrained to the use of suitably robust vessels that could come alongside the neighbouring rock face; and then loading could only be attempted on calm days. The whole endeavour was awkward, unpredictable, accident-prone, and slow.

The items of machinery that served the quarrying operation, and which are still standing in their original positions, date from the active period early in the 20th century. They provide an intriguing collection of items which make the quarry a site of industrial archaeology. The National Trust for Scotland intends to preserve this machinery. The foundations of quarrymen's dwellings stand on a grassy shelf above the quarry.

The current altar in the Abbey Church was made from Iona marble and was installed early in the 20th century, as was the lower part of the font. Iona marble was also chosen for the Kirk in Paris, St Andrew's Church in Jerusalem, and Crathie Church.

184. Creating a piece of distinctive Iona pottery

Craft Work

Iona was much more isolated in the 19th century than it is now, and the expectations of the islanders were more modest; but also they were more self-reliant. The production of cloth as a true cottage industry is one example: in 1840 there were seven families out of, perhaps, 60 on Iona, with their own hand-looms. The woven cloth they made was called 'Iona Tweed', and no doubt it was available to the two tailors on the island. Weaving was carried on until after the second world war.

We can detect a move from the manufacture of necessities towards the creation of luxuries by the end of the 19th century. The most notable exponent of the skills needed to satisfy the growing demand for luxury items from about 1898 was the versatile and inventive craftsman Alexander Ritchie who was supported in his art by his wife Euphemia. The Ritchies made exquisite pieces of silverware and jewellery that are prized today, and fashion items in several other materials; and they were also authors whose work included *'Iona Past and Present, with Maps'* and *'Map of Iona, with Sketch Historical and Geological of the Island'*. In 1994, 53 years after both died, the Iona Press published *'The Celtic Art of Iona, Drawings and Reproductions from the Manuscripts of the Late Alex Ritchie'*.

The two dominant skilled craft businesses on Iona today are wood sculpture, and pottery allied to watercolour painting and book illustration, each being pursued by a single individual whose work

185. Shuna Cottage which the Ritchies built in 1899

is highly regarded. In addition hand-knitting, marble carving, bee-keeping, shell-work and, until 1998, the cultivation of house plants, are all craft-hobbies through which residents are able to offer items for sale. And naturally Iona attracts visiting artists and photographers year after year.

186. Fashioning sought-after sculptures in wood

Many living in mainland Britain find themselves wondering about life on an island with a population of a little less than 100. Surely, they think, there must be serious deprivation, especially in winter: no resident doctor or nurse; deliveries of everything at the mercy of the weather; the high cost of produce; restricted choice, with a visit to the nearest supermarket needing a whole day; no street lighting.

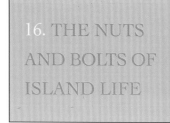

16. THE NUTS AND BOLTS OF ISLAND LIFE

187. Loch Staonaig, until recently the source of Iona's water

188. The village, Dun I, high ground and the Atlantic beyond

Actually, the style of Iona living is well-ordered and in some ways very attractive. The island's affairs are overseen by the Community Council made up of seven residents. In the local government structure the Community Council is part of the unitary authority Argyll & Bute Council, but it deals on some issues with the Argyll & Bute Area Office in Oban and for other, routine, matters with the Sub-Area Office in Tobermory. The topic of greatest importance to the islanders and therefore to the Community Council is the capacity, frequency, and reliability of the ferry service across the Sound of Iona - a service which has improved tremendously in recent years.

Transport on the Island is of lesser moment. Tourists do not bring vehicles across, and for many residents a car on Iona is almost an irrelevance. The 1991 census reported 32 cars amongst the 44

households on Iona. There are a few working vans, minibuses, and tractors; but congestion is absent.

189. Ferrying passengers to Iona from the steamer, about 1900, with just two oars!

Utilities and other services have been adapted to the need. The doctor from the Ross of Mull normally comes over for half a day a week, as does the nurse; the travelling dental service which pays visits to Fionnphort is used by the islanders. The police come if called, which is seldom. There is a proper post office, and a mail delivery system. Iona's Fire Station is by the jetty: the fire tender, when needed, is manned by part-time firemen resident on the island. The electricity supply is conventional. Gas comes in bottles, as on Mull, without problem. Water, which until 1996 was drawn from Loch Staonaig on Iona, is now piped from Loch Assopol, eight miles away on the Ross, in volumes and quality to meet growing expectations. There are weekly refuse collections. Telephones and mobile phones operate smoothly. There is a public library on Iona, albeit the smallest in Scotland, established in 1820.

The public road network on Iona consists of the single-track metalled road from the pier at the village following the east coast of the island, and also first to the south and then swinging west to strike across to the machair. All other roads are access tracks to houses, crofts and farms. The metalled road and the pier are the responsibility of Strathclyde Regional Council.

Domestic supplies from remote shops are not the problem that might be imagined. Ingenuity, and mutual collaboration, overcome the apparent difficulties. The shops on Iona obtain items not currently in stock with surprising speed: deliveries by one firm will often include purchases ordered from another. Routine provision of daily needs such as milk and newspapers follows streamlined channels.

To provide for visitors wanting to stay on Iona there are two hotels and at least 18 bed and breakfasts. Up to 90 guests a week stay with the Iona Community. There is also self-catering, some of which is taken year after year by the same people.

D r Samuel Johnson, on being carried over the surf to set foot on Iona in 1773, would have been hard pressed to have imagined the throngs that land on the island today. But have we reached saturation? And do we mind? In some respects the greater the numbers the greater the benefit to the island.

17. TRYING TO LOOK AHEAD

There are several influences tending to keep the numbers rising. In general people are becoming better able to visit the places that interest them - they enjoy increasing amounts of holiday during their working years, followed by longer spells of active retirement - and most have more money to spend on travel: each year quarter of a million holiday-makers return from Iona to recount their holiday experiences to their friends and neighbours, raising, however modestly, the overall level of awareness of the island: and the more impatient people on the mainland become with a life that feels overcrowded and tense, the more insistent is the lure of quiet, calm, open spaces. Should such haven happen to be enriched, as Iona is, by its sacred and cultural inheritance, and in addition be a picturesque island, we can be certain that it will always be irresistible.

Thus the number of visitors seems set to increase further if the mechanisms of travel can cope and, crucially, provided that tourism does not itself damage, or even destroy, the very delights that people are coming to savour.

The National Trust for Scotland has promulgated two aims, amplified by 14 detailed objectives, for the management of Iona. These

190. Inset above: Sunlight and shadows in the parish church

112

*191. Ben More on Mull
seen over Eilean nam Ban, from
village gardens on Iona*

aims and objectives apply to the whole island apart from the Abbey buildings, the Reilig Odhrain, and the Nunnery ruins. The aims are:

The Trust should ensure the permanent conservation, for the benefit of the nation, of Iona as a site of international importance in terms of history and archaeology and as an outstanding example of a Hebridean island landscape of high nature conservation value with an active crofting and farming population.

Sensitive to the extreme visitor pressure, the Trust should provide, and assist others to provide, for appropriate access to and appreciation of the island by the public. The provision of appropriate education and interpretation should be of the highest standard, sensitive to the qualities of the resource and the atmosphere of tranquillity and space for which Iona is renowned.

For the peace of mind of everyone who has relationship of any kind with the island we are glad to be able to report that, in addition to the fulfilment of these explicit aims of The National Trust for Scotland, the Abbey Church and other sacred buildings are constantly being maintained with care and skill by the Iona Cathedral Trust; and the financial health and continuity of the Iona Community are underwritten by the involvement of an enthusiastic body of Members, Associates, and Friends.

But, further, for the resident population the Isle of Iona needs to remain an attractive place in which to live and work for this and succeeding generations. There are issues of housing and house building, of schooling, of property tenure, and of other matters subject to regulation that bear upon people's contentment. Provided that there is consultation and progress on all these fronts, and that no far-reaching external event that impinges on the life of Iona occurs, we can be confident that the future of the island and its people is secure.

192. John Speed's 1610 map of the west coast of Scotland

THE DEUCALIDON SEA

C. Wrath or Faro head

Rona Iland
S. Rona

LEWYS
Nary
Neys
S. Columban
Bailm traid
S. Columbanus
Stornwaye caft
Stoy caft
L. Stornwaye
Radamach
Bailmes alg
Durna
L. Nofallo
Trufk
L. Erwin
S. Neald
S. Clement

Durneff
Ilen Handa
Gelleigueig
Bailnoheglis
The Stoir of Aſſin
Allerot Kikail

Stranavern
Colme
Drudon
Glenik
Tew
Ardurnes
Lavel
L. Naver
L. Rulſid
L. Glas
Laxford
Kil
Foillis
Stone
Kelſeing

Caithnes
Tounge ea
Com ca
Halladail
Far Strathy
Nermida
Strubbughter
Fore
Thurfo
Dunnet
Braul
L. Urdall
L. Caldel
Mayden papes
Baridail fl
Helmfdail
Helmsdail flu

Stratho Leith
Iners hin
Kyldon
Clinter filla
Browra
Clyne ea

Skyraflin
L. Aſſin
Rowra
Hilles of white marble of Roſſe
The marble mountaines of Sutherland
Ferne
Braymhat
Felag
Rogart
Clyne
Culmaly
Dunrobin caft

SUTHERLAND
Caſsarflu
Cillan flu
Strath
Carron flu
Claigan
Kean ea
Balnagonnes caft

Loch Brune
Esbrew
Ofill
Slew
Mera
Claight
Zutz
Brew
Salm
Mines of Iron
Lome

ROSSE
Hills of Allabaſter of Roſſe
Baile
Dingwall
Chanony
Rofemark
Red caft
Bewly Abbay

Tarbart
Tarbart
Tayn fl
Nyg
Cromarty flu
Cromar
Nardon
Tornwat caft

Fewris
L. Gar
Skoire
L. Refart
Culke
Dunra Toir
L. Hew

AſſinShire
Ardmanoth

Kair
Ardyrſeir
Kylrac caft

The Yles of Hebrides
Caled of Pliny
Hæbudes, of
Beda Meuaniae

Franta
Fladda
S. Nicolas
Allavik
Flodda
Trantnes
Tranternefca

SKYE
Dunbegan
Valternes
S. John
Bragdail
Knok fea
L. Enort
Dunfka ca
Tourean
Ay
Kiltir

Ellan Ronan
Allar towne
Ronaza
ſcalpa
Bruti allan
Stront caft
L. Drum
L. Lange
Kyntaile

Glenelg
L. Orne
The high moun-taynes of Ardmanoth

Lein
Louer caft
Inverneſs
Urquhart caft
Tray
Lochnes Moyn
Glennen Urquhart
Petty
Ranive
Boan caft
Soilles
Kr

MURAY
Calder ca
Tala
Kinguſy
Spey flu
Carry
Caſſ
Strath
Anar
Scarſi

Cannay
Rum
Egge
Muk

L. Newis
L. Errtord
Sell
L. Owin
Arfik
Tyren
Sell flu
Quhabyr
Bailniraid
Ardermouth head
Illean
Arrois ca
Bailmor
Lifmoir

LOQUHABER
La Sell
L. Zell
Culmaly
Leath
L. Loyne
Everlothea
Spanea flu
Matad
L. Olybe
L. Boyer
Foyre

L. Ark
L. Loyne
Leanny
Bad genoth
Badgenoth
L. Loche

La Garve
La Lake Neſſa are never froze
The Lake Neſſa are never froze
Grampian Mountain
Ellan Moy
Ruuon
Grumen flu
Ak
Frith flu

Brog
Collen
Scayl
Terrey
Ulway

Mu
L. Ayyryn
Cardeburg Caft
Lac Lephan
S. Eugenius
Colmkil or Iona Ile
Colmckil
Colonea
Oronza

Ia Cenylt
Dovart ca
Caruetei
L. Nawell
Efill
Terla
Tarbat
Skar iny

Loquhaber flor
Dunftafage ca
Bergonum ca
Stenbaftel Aw fl
Lorne
Broad Albayn
Lorne
Forlour fl
Eforlanca
Killeran

L. Leave
L. Long
Lomond hilles
Lac. Lomond
Brake Roody

L. Dicher
L. Loquhen
L. Lunell
Strath Amund
L. Lyon
Tay flu
L. Tay
Perth
L. Erne
Strath Erne
Innernyty ca

Athole
Blaire caft
Blaire
Dunke
Strat
Meſyn
Inche Chafra
Marpara fl
Drumnyrl la
Elpſton
Fulhtra

Sura
Sodore
S. Mathu
o. L. Weel
Terrey

Argile
L. Heke
Nadayn
L. Skriven
Reutiſar
S. Re.
yuiſa
Bruiy
Ofsir

Lennos
L. Gar
Rofnethy
Wagh Rofguy
Kilmoronak
Breſwell
Kilmarnoch
Monach ca.
Down caft
Kery
Menteith
Dunblain
Baquhider
Conbell
Clonon

L. Girvard
L. Arun
Crumecaft
Ila Iland
Gwebhal
Dunweg ca
Kylmany
Gegay

Bute
Reu.
thyiſa
Padway
Lamalaſhe
Arren Glenkil
Kyrk morich

Lennox
Dunbritoun
Glaiquo
Boſwell
Hamiltoun
Sterling
Struieling
Cothely

Wyfha
Naverſay
Karray
Kollaan
Gillieiaren
Pradda Ar
Dunoverf
Sandei

THE
Canal
The Mule of Cantyr

Brydyk
Androch ca
Dundonil
Caprintoun
Fail ab
Newmyll
Ayr
Kyle
Car
rike
Gudeen ca

Clidesdale
Avindalle ca
Douglas dale
Craufurdthouint ca
Lami
Anand

DOUGLAS dale

Malin
Coldagh haven
Portruſh
Dunluce
Skirries
Ship Iland
Whitehand
Dunſeeke
Tot
Tor Ile
Marketon bay
Forland
Tor bay

Ardunroun
Dariin
Ailhall
Coſegal
Bargaty
Blaquihan ca
Glenhope
Arſinfell
Beloch
Cragwell

Ochilree caft
Cumnok kirk
Craufurdmuir
Drufdeir
Saucher
Dumlanrick
Mortoun
Penpont
Nythes da le

GALLOWAY
The Mul of Galloway or the Mules nuke
Gregair
Wyghti
Coſwell
Kyphll
Salfei ab
L. Ryan
Gelenf ab

T OF IRELAND
Caft Corane
Caft Gowr
Lough Foyle

IRISH SEA

Anand
Hensel
Nenſel
Dunfres
Terricles
Finglandrig
Solua caft
Dundranam
The Hilles

Armit, I *Celtic Scotland* B T Batsford
  (Historic Scotland Series), (1997)

Boswell, J *Journal of a Tour to the Hebrides*
  (1786), OUP(1965)

Churchill, W S *A History of the English-speaking*
  Peoples (Vol I, Chapter 6) Cassell (1956)

Dunbar, J G and **Fisher, I** *The Iona Marble*
  Quarry HMSO (1988)

Eckstein, E *Historic Visitors to Mull, Iona &*
  Staffa Excalibur Press (1992)

Ferguson, R *Chasing the Wild Goose*
  Collins (1988)

Ferguson, R *George Macleod* Collins (1990)

Grierson, H J C *The Letters of Sir Walter Scott,*
  1808 - 1811 Constable & Co (1932)

Haswell-Smith, H *The Scottish Islands*
  Canongate Books (1996)

Hesketh, N *The Story of Mull and Iona*
  The Mercat Press, Edinburgh (1988)

Johnson, Dr S *A Journey to the Western Islands*
  of Scotland (1775), OUP (1965)

Laing, D *On the Present State of the Ruins of*
  Iona and their Preservation J Hughes,
  Edinburgh (1854)

Lilley, R K *Vegetation Management on Iona*
  University of Edinburgh

MacArthur, E M *Iona* Colin Baxter
  Photography (1997)

MacArthur, E M *Iona - The Living Memory*
  Edinburgh University Press

MacArthur, E M *Iona through Travellers' Eyes*
  New Iona Press (1991)

MacCormick, I *The Celtic Art of Iona,*
  Drawings and Reproductions from the
  Manuscripts of the Late Alex Ritchie
  The Iona Press (1994)

McLaren, M *The Highland Jaunt* Jarrolds,
  London (1954)

Maclean, L *A Historical Account of Iona*
  Stirling & Kennedy, Edinburgh (1833)

MacLeod, G *Shall We Rebuild?* Iona
  Community (1945)

Macquarrie, A *Iona through the Ages*
  Society of West Highland and Island
  Historical Research (1983)

Magnusson, M *Vikings!* The Bodley Head
  (1980)

Marsden, J *Sea-road of the Saints* Floris
  Books (1995)

Martin Martin *A Description of the Western Isles*
  of Scotland (c.1695) Birliun (1994)

Maxwell, W *Iona and the Ionians*
  Thos Murray & Son, Glasgow (1857)

Meehan, B *The Book of Kells* Thames and Hudson (1994)

Millar, J M *Flowers of Iona* New Iona Press (1993)

Millar, P W *Iona Pilgrim Guide* Canterbury Press (1997)

Murray, Hon Mrs A S *A Companion and Useful Guide to the Beauties in the West Highlands - Iona in 1802* London (1802)

Patterson, J L *Iona* John Murray, London (1987)

Prebble, J *The Lion in the North* Secker & Warburg (1971)

The Right Reverend the Bishop of the Isles *The Cathedral or Abbey Church of Iona* Day & Son, London (1866)

Ritchie, A *Iona* B T Batsford (Historic Scotland Series) (1997)

Ritchie, A and **Ritchie, E** *Iona Past and Present, with Maps* Geo Stewart & Co, Edinburgh (1934)

Ritchie, G and **Harman, M** (1985) *Exploring Scotland's Heritage - Argyll and the Western Isles* HMSO, Edinburgh

The Royal Commission on the Ancient and Historical Monuments of Scotland (1982) *Argyll - An Inventory of the Monuments, Volume 4 - Iona* HMSO, Edinburgh

193. Storm Island, and the Gribun cliffs on Mull, from the extreme north on Iona

The Royal Commission on the Ancient and Historical Monuments of Scotland (1993) *Iona* HMSO, Edinburgh

The Royal Commission on the Ancient and Historical Monuments of Scotland (1995) *Iona - A Guide to the Monuments* HMSO, Edinburgh

Saverin, T *The Brendan Voyage* BCA (1978)

Scott, Sir W *The Voyage of the Pharos* Scottish Library Association (1998)

Sharpe, R (Ed) *Adomnan of Iona - Life of St Columba* Penguin (1995)

Viner, D *The Iona Marble Quarry* The New Iona Press (1992)

Williams, G, Stowe, T and **Newton, A** *Action for Corncrakes* RSPB Conservation Review 5 (1991)

Wilson, R *Columba of Iona, Island Soldier* Hall the Printer (1935)

The artists whose work is reproduced in this book have each been kind enough to say what it is about Iona, in providing its diverse subjects for painting, that especially appeals to them and how it affects their work.

Jan Fisher

'Every time I visit Iona new visual experiences reveal aspects of the island previously unseen, like watching its personality develop. The time of year and the time of day, the direction of the wind, the state of the tides, sunshine and storms and the colour of the light, all contribute to infinite variations on a familiar scene. Every bay has its own special rocks sculptured by the waves, some glittering with jewel-like colours, others glistening jet-black rising from white sand or turbulent seas. And the sea, itself a challenge for a lifetime's work.'

Pat Malpas

'I took early retirement from teaching to concentrate on my life-long interest in painting. I first visited Iona in 1995, and immediately fell under its spell. Dark rock forms rise from white sand which gleams in certain lights; the skies can change from

brilliant blue to brooding grey; the surrounding waters, streaked with turquoise, throw up plumes of white foam; all this gives the island a magical air. Despite being battered by the elements the island remains a quiet centre of spirituality and inspiration.'

Gordon Menzies

'Since I established the Iona Pottery in 1982 I have tried to reflect the feeling of Iona through colour in painting and pottery. I have been mainly using pastel for my seascapes, and more recently watercolour. Expansion into publishing has been a good development through limited edition prints and postcards covering the work of Cadell, Peploe, Duncan and Glass: this group of images is known as the Iona Collection. My pottery is an extension of my painting, reflecting not only the colours of the sea and the sky but also the texture and feel of the rocks.'

Tom Shanks

'I began my love affair for drawing the West Highland landscape as a boy during holidays in Skye in 1929 and 1930. These holidays had a profound effect on my work, both emotionally and nostalgically. The landscapes, the villages and the island itself had an atmosphere at that time that no longer exists - an essence of mystery and loneliness in wild headlands, mountains and moorlands. That essence is what I try to capture in my paintings. When I go north from Glasgow to the hills and the islands I see them with a fresh eye every time, and with greater wonder and appreciation.'

Julia Wroughton

Julia Wroughton ran the Inniemore School of Painting at Carsaig on the south coast of the Ross of Mull for 30 years, from 1968 to 1998. Not only is she a highly accomplished and prolific artist with many exhibitions to her credit, but she has also introduced large numbers of her students on residential courses at Inniemore to the Isle of Iona. Of her own paintings of Iona she says:

'Having lived on Mull, and painted on Mull and Iona, for so long I have developed a special attraction to Iona where the light on the landscape and the farm buildings is exceptional, exerting a strong pull on me.'

195. Overleaf: Autumn sunrise over the Sound of Iona from the summit of Dun I

194. Jan Fisher's watercolour of Iona - the North End

119

INDEX

Abbey 9, 18, 23, 31, 37, 39, 42, 58
Abbey Church 23, 31-33, 50,
    52, 57, 60, 99, 114
Abbot of Iona 27
Adomnan 18
Anderson, Robert, Sir 50
Anglo-Saxons 37
Antrim 15
Argyll 15, 53
Argyll & Bute Council 110
Argyll and Sutherland
    Highlanders 54
Argyll, Dukes of 50
Argyll, Earls of 50
Argyll, 5th Duke of 46
Argyll, 8th Duke of 23, 50, 52, 53
Argyll, 10th Duke of 9, 95
Assopol, Loch 111
Atholl 22
Atlantic Ocean 17, 25
Augustine of Hippo 37
Augustinian order 36, 40

Baile Mor 66
Bannockburn 33
Bay at the Back of
    the Ocean 63, 69, 70
Benedictine 29, 31, 32, 36, 58, 66
birds 82-92
Bishop's House 18, 100
bones 13
Boswell, James 43
Brendan, Saint 17
Bridei, King 21
Bronze age 12
Bruce, Robert 33
Bull Hole 63
Bunessan 62

Cairn of the Back to Ireland 18
Caithness 27
Calva 69
Cambrensis, Giraldus 19
Campbells 50
Canterbury, Archbishop of 37
Carsaig 31

Cathedral 31
Celts 12, 15
Census, 1991 96
centenary, fourteenth 23
centenary, thirteenth 23
Christianity 15, 21, 58
Clan Donald 29
clay 13
climate 12
coast, Biscay 25
coast, English 25
coast, French 25
coast, Russian 25
Coffee Shop 18
Columba, Saint 9, 16-18,
    21-24, 29, 47, 100
Community Council 110
Connal 21
Coracle 17
coracle 17
Culloden 101

Dalriada 15, 21
Daniell, William 49
Denmark 24
Disruption 100
Donegal, County 16
Dorchester 27
Dublin, Trinity College 27
Dunadd 15
Dun Bhuirg 12, 13, 69
Dunkeld 32
Dun I 13, 56
Durrow 22
Dutchman's Cap 62

East End 66
Eilean nam Ban 31, 62
Episcopalians 100
Erraid 62

Fair Isle 95
Feldspar-rock 63
Fetlar 95
Fife 22
Fingalton Mill 56

Fionnphort 23, 62
fishing 98
Fladda 62
Flanders 54
flowers 72-77
Foula 94
Free Church 100
Fuinary 54

Gartan 16
geology 64
Glasgow 55, 59, 104
Gokstad 24
golf 106
Gospel, St Mark's 19
Gospel, St Luke's 16
Govan 55, 56, 59
Graham, H D 82, 105
Grampians 22
Grasspoint 47
Great Glen 21, 29
Grenadier, PS 23

Harald, King 27
Harold, King 27
Hebrides 12, 22, 29, 63, 72
Herbs 30
Heritage Centre 67, 99
Hermit's Cell 13, 56
Highlands 29, 49, 99
Hugh Fraser Foundation 9, 95

Information Point 23
Inverness 21
Iona Cathedral Trust 114
Iona Cathedral Trustees 50, 56
Iona Community 17, 54, 55, 57-59, 111
Iona Heritage Trust 99
Ireland 9, 15-18, 22, 23

Jacobites 101
James, King 19
Johnson, Samuel, Dr 43, 112
Justice Carpet 52

Keats, John 47
Kells 27, 29
Kells, Book of 21, 27
kelp 101
Kilmartin 15
kings, Irish 31
kings, Norwegian 31
kings, Scottish 31
Kirk, the 99
Knox, John 33

Lewisian Gneiss 63
Lindisfarne 27
Llanfairisgaer 23
Lochaline 54
London 49
longships, Viking 24, 25
Lordship of the Isles 29

Macbeth 45
Macdonald of Staffa 45
MacBrayne, David 23
machair 66, 67
MacLean's Cross 32
MacLeod Centre 18, 58
MacLeod, Lord 23, 54-58, 60
marble 63, 70, 106, 107
marine life 78-81
Martin, Martin 42, 43
Martyrs' Bay 27, 31, 68, 100
Mediterranean 26
Mendelssohn, Felix 48
Moderator of the
    General Assembly 50, 54, 57
monks 99
Morven 54
Mull, Isle of 12, 62, 65, 72
Museum of Scotland, New 33

National Trust for Scotland, The 9, 63,
    76, 95, 96, 103, 112, 114
Neolithic age 12
Norman Conquest 29
Northern Ireland 15

Northern Lights, Commissioners of 47
Northumbria 22
Norway 24
Nunnery 36, 39, 40, 42, 56
nuns 22, 101, 104

O

Oban 22, 101, 104
Oriel College 54
Orkney Islands 27
Out Skerries 95

P

pagan practices 15
Papa Stour 95
Paris 25
Parish Church 32, 100
Patrick, Saint 16
Perth 36
Perugia 29
Picts 15
population 94, 96
Port Ban 69
Port of the Coracle 17, 69
pottery 108
Presbyterian Church 100

Q

Queen, HM The 57
Queen Mother, HM The 57

R

raised beaches 66, 69
Reformation 23, 31, 33
Reginald 29, 37
Reilig Odhrain 30, 31, 56, 114
Reliquary, Monymusk 32
Ritchie, Alex and Euphemia 108, 109
Road of the Dead 31
Robinson, Mary 23
Roman army 16
Roman Catholics 23, 100
Ross, Easter 22
Ross of Mull 15, 18, 31

S

Saint Columba's Bay 68, 70

Saint Columba's Shrine 32
Saint Cuthbert's Church 55
Saint Giles Cathedral 54
Saint John's Cross 29, 31, 32
Saint Martin's Cross 32, 56
Saint Ninian's Isle 65
Saint Oran's Chapel 30
Saint Ronan's Bay 68, 104
Saint Ronan's Church 40
Salonika 54
Sandeels Bay 68
Scandinavia 24
Scots 15
Scott, Walter, Sir 45, 46
sheep 103
Shellfish 98
Shetland Islands 27, 65
Skerryvore 47
Skye 72
Soa 65
Somerled 29
Sound of Iona 9, 18, 23, 31, 63, 98, 104
Spouting Cave 70
Staffa 62

Stamford Bridge 27
standing stones 15
Staonaig, Loch 56, 66, 70
Storm Island 25, 65
Strathclyde Regional Council 111
Sweden 24
Sweyne, the 47

T

Tayside 21
Telford, Thomas 99
Thistle Camps 9, 70
Tobermory 78, 110
Toc H 55
tombolo 25, 65
Torran Rocks 62
Torr Mor 31
Treshnish Isles 62

U

Ullapool 29
Ulva 95, 99

V

vallum 18, 30
Victoria, Queen 48, 104
Vikings 17, 21, 24, 26, 27, 29
Vulgate text,
    Saint Jerome's 21

W

West End 66
White Strand of the
    Monks 27, 65, 68
Wild Goose Publications 59
Winchester College 54

Y

yews 12
York 27

Z

Zetland 47

196. Part of the Nunnery Wall